# How to Be
# a Happy Parent . . .
# in Spite of
# Your Children!

Anne & Andrew -

Behave!

JL Spn

ALSO BY FRED G. GOSMAN

Spoiled Rotten:
Today's Children and How to Change Them

# How to Be
# a Happy Parent . . .
# in Spite of
# Your Children!

## FRED G. GOSMAN

VILLARD BOOKS

NEW YORK

1995

Villard Books is a registered trademark of Random House, Inc.

Library of Congress Cataloging-in-Publication Data

Gosman, Fred G.
How to be a happy parent ... in spite of your children! / by Fred G. Gosman.
p. cm.
ISBN 0-679-43334-1
1. Child rearing—United States. 2. Parenting—United States.
3. Parent and child—United States. I. Title.
HQ769.G6988 1995
649'.1—dc20 94-27676

Manufactured in the United States of America on acid-free paper

9 8 7 6 5 4 3 2
First Edition
Book design by Jo Anne Metsch

*To Bob and Mike,*
*with unconditional and everlasting love*

# Contents

## CONTENTS

# Introduction

WHEN DID PARENTING BECOME SUCH work?

Used to be, it was taken for granted. Moms and dads just did it. Unthinkingly. Naturally. Successfully.

You'd bring a baby home from the hospital, warm a bottle or two, throw some store-bought applesauce in a dish, point the little fellow in the general direction of grade school, and all would usually turn out fine. Heck, the lad was even *grateful*, and had the decency to move out of the house about when he was expected to.

We have become unsure of the rules and unsure of our roles. Parenting, like brain surgery, is now all-consuming, fraught with anxiety, worry, and self-doubt.

We have allowed what used to be simple and natural to become bewildering and intimidating.

We do so much for our children, yet worry if it's enough. We develop arthritis from pushing the swing and cataracts from looking for Waldo. Our daughter eats waffles shaped like Mickey Mouse, and our son eats Turtles pasta but, increasingly, we don't feel like superheroes.

Today we have more information but less confidence. Fewer kids but more fears. More sacrifices but greater guilt. And everything is complex.

One couple recently invested $40 in baby-naming software that listed 14,000 names. Know what they agreed to, after three fights and two weeks without talking to each other? Jim.

Recently, I was a guest on a talk show, and a thirty-five-year-old married man called in with a terribly sad comment. He was so upset by all the trouble his friends were having with their children that he decided not to have any. Has parenting really become such a hassle, such a burden, that adults who claim to love children are dropping out?

Finding the perfect balance is getting harder

and harder. We need to teach our children to be cautious without imparting fear, to learn right from wrong without being judgmental, to be assertive but not pushy, to stick to routines without sacrificing spontaneity, and to be determined but not stubborn.

Some of us have begun to crack under the pressure, displaying such predictable signs of acute emotional distress as short-temperedness and repeating our parents' clichés. Certainly, new forces confront us, such as hurried lives, working moms, the prevalence of divorce, and the influence of the media. Expletives are no longer deleted. Our daughters wear letter jackets and become doctors and lawyers. Our sons ask which earring goes best with their outfit.

But simply because our times are complex, does it follow that our parenting must also be? Must we reject the common sense that worked so well in the past just because our times are high-tech? We live in such fear of being called "old-fashioned" that we are cutting ourselves off from that which is proven.

I need to point out here that I am certainly not claiming any kind of infallibility. Heck, I'm not even an expert—just an everyday dad, father to

Bob and Mike. I have no meaningful initials after my name, no Ph.D., M.D., or M.S.W. Not to worry completely, I did spend a week in school recently and now have advanced certification. I am proud to say I am a C.F.R.H. Never heard of it? Don't fear. It's on the cutting edge of modern parenting theory. C.F.R.H.—Concerned Father with a Receding Hairline.

From the success of my first book, *Spoiled Rotten*, as well as from speaking before and meeting with thousands of fellow parents, I have learned that we have much in common. We are all struggling to find the proper balance between gift giving and indulgence, freedom and license, spontaneity and accountability. We don't want to become *clones* of our parents, yet we are growing increasingly tired of reasoning with two-year-olds. And are ripe for change.

In *How to Be a Happy Parent . . . in Spite of Your Children!*, I've tried to suggest a middle path, synthesizing my ideas with those of the thousands of parents who were kind enough to volunteer the details of their success.

The combined parent power out there is *enormous.* A dad in Illinois used a simple phone book to cut his child's toy requests by nearly 90 percent.

INTRODUCTION

A mom in Michigan used seven little words to halt the perpetual misbehavior of her middle-schooler. A California mom ended the nightly battle over television. A Maryland mother brought her daughter's clothing purchases under control. A Massachusetts mom finally got the help around the house that she deserved. A Michigan family reduced sibling rivalry to manageable levels. And a Missouri couple actually enjoys mealtime.

Too often we think it is pompous to let others know what is working effectively for us. Ridiculous. It's kind, and downright helpful. We tell our kids to share. Adults can, too.

Some of the suggestions I pass on here may be perfect for your family, others may not. *That is as it should be!* One person's bribe is another's reward. Every family is different and has its own personality and values. People of goodwill may well differ on the merits of using fines as punishment or denying soccer practice to a misbehaving child. But at least let's see how some of these approaches work in other homes. The more strategies we close our minds to, the fewer we have at our disposal.

We must return optimism to our parenting. Quickly! To focus on the joys, not the hassles; the love, not the disappointments; the common sense, not the complexities.

By utilizing our shared strength and resources, we can help each other, support each other, and return to our homes the calm, the peace, and the joy that we all so deeply deserve.

# How to Be
# a Happy Parent . . .
# in Spite of
# Your Children!

# Growing Things Need a Good Root System

THE OTHER DAY I WAS WALKING OUT OF MY house at the exact instant a mother passed by, pushing a stroller. I looked at the child and commented, "That's the cutest baby I've ever seen." I loved the mom's response. Without skipping a beat, she responded, "Isn't she?"

Our little ones are *so* precious, so innocent. What a responsibility! What an opportunity!

We must pay our dues with our children and make them a priority. Marvel at their every movement. Comfort them unceasingly when they are ill. Call forth that extra degree of patience when none is left. Make time for them. That's how bonding occurs, I think. Sacrificing. Nurturing. Worrying.

Ignore them at your peril! A Connecticut mom learned this lesson in a humorous but embarrassing way. She was with her three-year-old at the post office. The child wanted her attention, but Mom kept saying, "Just a minute." The child reached up and pulled on Mom's skirt. It fell to the ground. There was Mom in the middle of the post office showing off her oldest slip. "The next time we were out," she says, "I answered his questions real quick."

All we can give our kids is time. They're what matters. Read them the comics on Sunday morning. Praise them often. It's a shame our day-planners don't come preprogrammed with time set aside for kids.

Not that we won't inflict a minor disaster or two upon them. I made a "minor" error when I was teaching Bob how to bike. The newsboy passed near us, and I took the paper from him so he wouldn't have to walk it to our door. The problem was that Bob was six feet from an intersection and we hadn't yet covered braking!

Mike perpetually reminds me of the time I almost "killed" him with a baseball. We had gone to the park so he could practice his hitting, but forgot to bring the batting helmet (we were using a hard ball). Mike kept begging and begging for me to pitch anyway, real slowly. I made a poor decision and decided to throw one in. Perhaps it was traveling two miles an hour! Mike somehow managed to allow the ball to hit him in the head. Nothing like beaning your own child to make a father feel proud.

Many families make sure special family time is structured into their day. A Michigan mom puts her daughter down fifteen minutes early. She lies on the bed, too, and just relaxes and talks with her daughter. "There are no interruptions, and the day ends on a loving note."

A mom with twins got tired of each child seeking her exclusive attention before bedtime. So the kids alternate. Mom engages one of the girls in a one-on-one activity for fifteen minutes before bedtime while the other child reads. And the next day it's reversed. She says the kids *love* it.

Some families literally block out time for family. A Texas couple puts a DO NOT DISTURB sign on their front door from one to four on Sunday afternoons. No friends are allowed to drop in. Seems funny at first, but shouldn't more of us be fighting to protect family time?

A Florida couple with three children schedules a special two-hour period each week for one of their children to be with either Mom or Dad. They do simple things, like hiking, bike riding, or going to the mall. "Each child thoroughly enjoys it; they all look forward to *their* time."

A Colorado couple has "Friday Night Safari." One child plans the outing with one of the parents, and no one else knows what is planned. An Arkansas family makes a big deal out of going to the mall. Though they normally restrict such visits, they have a semiannual "Shopping Spree!" Kids go wild. Nifty names can go a long way to enhance otherwise ordinary activities. How about "Ballpark Bash"? "Fabulous Friday"? "Affordable Tuesday"? Whatever we call them, at least we'll be together with our children.

A Pennsylvania mom has an annual "Mommy and Me" day with each child. They go out to lunch and spend the afternoon shopping or at the movies. The children maintain a special book in which they record the details of each year's outing. A Vermont family has a special book where kids' absurd explanations for misdeeds are recorded for posterity. You might keep a large box available as a "Family History File." Throw in everything of potential interest—receipts for the first birthday cake or pair of big-boy pants; your daughter's report cards or artwork. What a joy to look at someday (and what a treat for your child's spouse!).

Start some inexpensive traditions. I sat next to a lady on a plane who said she kept the yearly birthday newspaper for each family member. What a neat thing, to see your special pile grow year after year. What a sense of growth and continuity. And a California family has a special family song, written by the kids, sung only on special family occasions. Even if the older kids might think it corny, what memories!

Be zany with the kids. Just because we're the parents doesn't mean we can't have fun and occasionally be outrageous. If your son is traveling out of the country with an aunt, fax a hello to him at his hotel. Have an occasional water fight with your daughter when she's young (and your spouse is out)! Play tackle football in the snow—your legs will defrost eventually.

Once I learned about a ridiculously low airfare

between Chicago and Kansas City, maybe nineteen bucks each way. I flew there with Mike for one of his birthdays. Sure, with the car rental, the day was not cheap. But neither are two or three video games. And here we had memories.

The great home-run hitter Harmon Killebrew recalls how his mother always complained about the boys playing baseball on the front lawn. But Dad came through, he recalls. "We're not raising grass here," he would say. "We're raising boys."

I'm a little upset about all the resorts that now advertise the possibility of having a wonderful family vacation without ever seeing the kids. "He'll be in supervised play, with kids *his own age*." Big deal! There's a name for a place like that—school.

The ads are more and more brazen all the time. One promises that your child will fly down on a separate plane. Another guarantees that your children will never be on the same island. Sure, all these programs have great employees. But kids need parents, not staff.

Returning from one of these "family" vacations can be a true revelation. Grandma asks, "How was the fishing?"

The child says, "Terrific! I caught a shark." The

father responds, "Nobody in my party caught a thing."

"How was the snorkeling?"

"Horrible," the child says. "It wasn't clear at all on Tuesday." "Terrific," the mom says. "What a beautiful Thursday."

"How was the food?" the perplexed grandma ventures.

"Horrible," says the kid. "Hot dogs weren't good. Even the waiters were rude." "Great," says Mom. "A Napoleon to die for. And what service!"

Be there, too, at the times in your child's life when he needs to put forth effort.

We can't stress reading enough. Let the children see *us* read and hear *us* talking about books. Take the little ones to the library often and read to them as much as possible.

I absolutely love how a Florida family encourages reading. The parents make a *big* deal out of each child getting the library card. The family comes over for a special dinner. A picture of the child receiving his library card is sent to the out-of-town grandparents. Aunts and uncles chip in for a gift certificate to a local bookstore. What a send-off!

Active involvement with the child's education is a must. Attendance at conferences is critical. For both Mom and Dad, if possible. Even if the sitter is an unplanned expense, so what? Rent movies the following Saturday night. What a glorious way to stress the importance of education to your child.

We should never underestimate the impact of our words. We can yell and scream, demean, or react calmly and gracefully when confronted with minor crises. Kids are so impressionable, and our words have such impact.

An Upstate New York mom, visiting friends, told her misbehaving six-year-old that he would have to walk home (six miles) if he continued to misbehave. Suddenly, the mother noticed that her son was missing. After searching the nearby neighborhood for twenty minutes, she called 911, and a formal search was organized. The child was finally found two miles from home. "What were you doing?" Mom angrily inquired. Replied the son, "I misbehaved, and thought I'd get a head start!"

Be slow to condemn. We spill our wine occasionally; why wouldn't the kids spill their milk?

HOW TO BE A HAPPY PARENT

Most problems work themselves out; the fewer labels we put on our children, the better.

My three-year-old son Bob once gave us a not inconsiderable challenge. We had just concluded brunch in a fancy restaurant, and on his way out, he went up to every table he passed and very clearly said, "Goddamn it." What to do? We ignored his actions and hoped they wouldn't recur. We feared that a long lecture might just reinforce his behavior. Fortunately, our intuition was correct, though I do fear that two elderly waitresses have yet to recover!

An artistic three-year-old excitedly came running up to his father and begged him to come see the "pretty new picture" in his room. Dad feared and found the worst: The child had used his crayons and drawn a gigantic mural on his bedroom wall. What did Dad do? Explode? Throw away the crayons? Not at all. He realized he never had told his child not to write on walls. The child *meant* well. So Dad praised the drawing, even though he quickly informed his child of the advantages of using paper.

A seven-year-old was collecting soup labels for his elementary school and got carried away, soaking the labels off all the unopened soup cans in the cupboard. Did Mom throw a tantrum? Of course not. No way. She inaugurated a cute tradition, now beginning its fifteenth year. Tuesday is "Soup Surprise" night.

What to do if you make a mistake with your kids? Simple. Apologize. That's what we tell *them* to do. The more reasonable *we* are, the more cooperation we will get.

And allow things to work *both* ways. Recently, I came home an hour later than I had told Mike I would. He was even asleep when I returned. But the next morning I told him I had "violated" curfew, and took three dollars off the amount he owes me in our ongoing gin-rummy game.

Let kids win an argument occasionally, especially when they're *correct*. Mike tried to con me out of some golf balls some years back, and in the process won the day.

I had called from out of town, and Mike said, "There's some stuff in the rummage area I would like. That would be okay, wouldn't it?"

"Sure, Mike," I said. "But, tell me. What is the stuff?"

"You know, just stuff you'll sell for pennies on

the dollar at our next rummage sale. I could have it, couldn't I?"

"Probably," I said. "But, Mike, what is it?"

"Twelve new golf balls," he responded. Mistakenly, I had placed them in the rummage area.

"Mike," I said. "You've just begun to play golf. You don't need *new* golf balls for the short little par-three courses you play. Your brother and I play bigger courses. We'll need them. Sorry, but you can't have the balls."

Then Mike hit me with the zinger. "That's okay, I'll live with your decision, but isn't it ironic? You play courses with lots of trees and water hazards and lose lots of balls, yet you need *new* ones. I never lose a ball on my shorter courses, and I have to use *old* ones."

I was struck by the cogency of his argument. I still don't have a good answer. So I said, "Mike, if I give you three of the balls, will you end this conversation and let me talk to Mom?"

Thankfully, he said, "Yes." To this day I feel I got off cheap.

Children grow up so quickly; we must pay our dues when they are young. The tricycle will be sold at rummage before you know it. Your son, who you thought would turn into a Spaghetti-O, will ask for a second steak. The child who couldn't sleep through the night will awaken at noon.

We can't even take their kisses for granted. I had a sad day a while back. I was leaving for a speaking trip, and for the first time, I left the house without a kiss from at least one of my boys. Suddenly, it just didn't flow. It was unnatural. I settled for a manly, "Take good care of your mother."

They used to fight for my kisses. Now they are history. Not their fault. Just the way things often are between dads and sons. But it was one of the saddest days of my life. You fathers of daughters are lucky. You'll get kisses the rest of your life.

We must constantly tell our children that we love them—with our voice, not just with our actions. Men especially need to communicate. To tell people years after the fact that they were the priority is the coward's way. If men can muster the courage to fire an employee, tell off a boss, or assume financial risk, they can dig deep and say the three little words their wives and children need to hear.

We must all say these words. Repeatedly. Incessantly. Shamelessly. Daily. Purchases don't express it. Indulgence doesn't express it. Only expressing it expresses it.

Accepting, permanent, irrevocable love. A love for a child despite his flaws, despite her sins. A love that doesn't fluctuate with grade-point or batting averages. A love for them just the way they are.

To love them gay, or any way—single, divorced, married, intermarried. To love them wealthy or needy, religious or agnostic, drinker or teetolater, scholar or charmer, fat or small, bulimic or anorexic, calm or frenetic, sane or schizophrenic.

Never underestimate the impact of stating your love. A Midwestern dad routinely said "I love you" to his child before bedtime. One night he forgot and went downstairs to watch TV. Within minutes his child came running down and threw his arms around his father. With tears streaming down his face, he said, "Daddy, we forgot our 'I love you's."

I am not an exceptionally spiritual man, but I must confess to believing something that would be hard to explain rationally. I think every time a parent says *I love you* to a child, he is helping to create a protective barrier that will shield his loved one from some of the earth's occasional pain, that provides encouragement when self-esteem falters, that gives hope when, otherwise, pessimism would reign.

Imagine your house is on fire. The kids are out safe. You have a chance to save one thing. There's the TV set, and there's the family history file—with all the baby pictures, Sarah's first tooth, Jason's bronzed baby shoes, the Mother's and Father's Day cards. Which do you go for?

Simple, right? What could be more precious than that little one we helped create? We must nurture him. We must set good examples. We have to give him our time. And we must express our love.

He's the best of "us," and deserves nothing less.

## POINTS TO REMEMBER

- Parenting doesn't end at conception.

- It's hard to have a *family* vacation when the resort promises a ten-dollar rebate every time you see your child.

## HOW TO BE A HAPPY PARENT

- There is *no* excuse for never saying *I love you* to your child.

- The only thing of true value a parent can give a child is time.

- Parents who refuse to make their children a priority shouldn't have any.

- There are few things as important as instilling a sense of humor in your children.

- The more reasonable the parent, the less frequent the misbehavior.

- No one ever looks back and says he wishes he would have spent *less* time with his children.

# Children Should Learn to Use a Potty Before Mastering a Slide Rule

WHAT EVER HAPPENED TO FREE TIME?

Used to be, kids could relax. Make their own plans. Veg out. Suck a good thumb.

No longer. Now they're on the go all the time. Traditionally, when a woman learned she was pregnant, the first call was to the father. Now it's to the admissions office at Computer Tots. Pretty soon, the first words of many of our young will be *car pool.*

It is easy to defend all these early activities individually, of course. "Music is important to my family." "Gymnastics will develop self-esteem." "The discipline of competitive swimming will do my six-year-old good." All so true. But aren't there advantages to play time—glorious, simple play time, unstructured and free?

Dewar's scotch has its famed "Dewar's Profile." We have one, too, of a baby doer:

### Doer's Profile

| | |
|---|---|
| Diaper: | Designer |
| Favorite Beverage: | Enfamil Sports Drink |
| Latest Book: | *The Cat in the Hat* (in French) |
| Favorite Instrument: | Tie: Flute, viola |
| Latest Accomplishment: | Memorized Childcraft |
| After-school Activity: | Pre-pre-pre-pre-pre-SAT |
| Profile: | QUIET |
| | COMMITTED |
| | POTTY-TRAINED |

Classes, classes, classes. Soccer this. Music that. Swimming now, anyhow.

Kids no longer know how to fill time themselves. The Olsons recently told Brian he could enjoy an afternoon of leisure:

"Who will drive me there?" he inquired.

"No one, dear," Mom replied. "You'll relax and think of things to do around the house."

"When may I expect my progress report?" Brian asked.

"There isn't any," Dad responded. "You aren't being graded at all."

"Well, what should I do?" Brian questioned.

"Anything you want," his parents replied. "Read a book. Go outside. Play in the playroom."

"Think I'll do the latter," Brian responded. "Will one of you be kind enough to show me where it is?"

Hectic schedules create all kinds of problems. Grandmother had to wait an hour and a half for her grandchild's first birthday party to begin; the violin lesson ran late. One grandfather asked his daughter when his grandson's soccer game would be over and dropped in an hour afterward. He was surprised that his grandson wasn't home. How was he to know the game was being played three states north?

Just registering for all the different classes becomes a full-time occupation. Status used to go to those who had the largest home; now it goes to the child who is on the most waiting lists.

We hurry our children so. The Clarksons sued their local soccer league, upset by the rule that members of the traveling squad had to be potty-trained. And the Mastersons charged the Wrights with "influence peddling." They distributed free Wet Ones wipes at day care, just four days before their daughter narrowly defeated their own for class president.

Soon the bandwagon effect takes hold. If all the neighborhood kids are enrolled in nursery school, whom will your daughter play with if you elect to keep her at home? If the Smiths' child is in pre-hockey or pre-math, ours must be also. We don't want our youngster falling behind. Your daughter loves tennis and asks the neighbor girl to play. She declines, having been at tennis camp all day. Soon we enroll our daughter. It's the only way she can get up a game.

Stranger and stranger things occur daily. The Walerstein girl didn't start to walk until she was three years old. Of course, there were mitigating circumstances—she was learning on a six-foot-long balance beam. And the Petermans had to move out of their subdivision. Their high-schooler failed to make the National Honor Society, their third grader reads like a third grader, and the four-year-old isn't even multilingual.

We lose sight of the fact that kids develop on different schedules. The second-grade home-run king may not make his high school team. Your five-year-old daughter, the fast runner, may be a slow middle-schooler. Very often the children who truly excel come out of nowhere, developing their interests and abilities at a slower initial rate than their peers.

It's funny how you never meet a parent who rushes his child. That's what *other* parents do. All we are doing is reacting to our child's "natural" ability. Our daughter smiles during reruns of *Mr. Ed* and is dispatched to riding camp. Our son bumps into a chess set and is proclaimed a prodigy.

Many of us *live* through our kids. We wished we could have danced, so our daughter is in pre-ballet whether she likes it or not. Mike Krzyzewski, head basketball coach at Duke University, recently observed that "there are more people living their lives through their kids now than there ever were when I grew up. There are a lot of losers to that."

A very smart dad saw through this trap. He loved baseball and excitedly asked his son if he was looking forward to playing T-ball again. The child responded, "No way, Dad. I played that *last* summer." Dad was crushed, but realized the less he persisted, the more likely that his son would return to the game.

How many of us have such wisdom? Thousands of parents dispatch their children to year-round tennis camps, hoping they become superstars. Didn't we used to condemn the East Germans for identifying talent early and forcing kids to live away from home? We justify the expense by saying, "We'll ensure a college scholarship." But if the camp costs $20,000 each and every year, aren't we financially behind regardless?

A Midwestern dad is prepared to change jobs and move to one of the coasts so his daughter (one of several children) can get the best coaching. "We want to treat her passions seriously," he says. I don't know. What about the disruption to the family? Making the other children move? Not being around Grandma, aunts and uncles, cousins, and friends?

Many sports professionals have suggested taking a closer look at our priorities. James Loehr, director of sports science for the United States Tennis Association, has long advocated abolishing national championships and rankings for tennis players twelve and under. "Adults can't deal with that pressure. How can kids?" And the soccer coach of Old Dominion University has referred to the practice of sending under-ten travel teams to other states as "kind of scary."

Isn't there a downside when we rush our kids? A large study at Michigan State University found that the earlier a child starts a sports activity, the earlier he drops out. And a sports psychologist who works with some Atlanta Braves ballplayers reports "tons of calls" from parents who request over-the-counter drugs to help their children regain their "killer instinct."

Kids often *resent* all these activities. David Elkind, the marvelous psychologist who authored *The Hurried Child*, reports that one ten-year-old was scratching his skin raw. The problem disappeared when the parents cut back on his activities. Other psychologists have noted that children sometimes believe parents arrange so many activities so they don't have to spend time with them.

A child in numerous soccer leagues was practically *happy* to be injured. "Got to rest," he said. And a teacher at a prestigious Montessori school wrote that she saw many children burned out on the alphabet and dinosaurs by age four. "They literally lost any wonder about the world, because they had been exposed to so much of it already."

If *all* the kids are doing an activity, no one is gaining a competitive benefit. Look at the various SAT-review courses. At select colleges, probably almost all the applicants take them. They therefore don't really help differentiate one applicant from another. All that's happened is there is an additional financial burden for the parents and greater pressures for our teenagers.

Recently, an article appeared in the paper about an eleven-year-old girl who set the record for being the youngest female to fly across the country. "This is something she'll never, ever be able to forget," her mother is quoted as saying. I'm sure this is true. But what can she do for an encore?

Likewise with a recent bar mitzvah. The child wrote software for his own video game, and his parents had it manufactured. It cost about $10,000. All very laudable, but isn't reading from the Bible supposed to be the focus of attention?

I recently came upon a book called *How to Multiply Your Baby's Intelligence*, and it made me rather sad. Inside was a picture of a twenty-month-old child. He reads five thousand words and dozens of homemade books. He knows over five thousand bits of intelligence about birds, fish, reptiles, insects, presidents, world leaders, U.S. states, European and African countries, star constellations, human anatomy, mechanical science, and great art masterpieces. He plays the violin, knows several hundred Japanese kanji, and is an "instant" mathematician, handling arithmetic, geometry, and algebra.

Give me a break! What are we doing to our kids? Tell me something important. How is he at "Itsy-Bitsy-Spider"? Does he know which little piggy ate the roast beef?

I think it's scary for kids to hit their pinnacle when they are young. What have they to look forward to? Children need a sense of wonder, a sense of anticipation, of unfolding. If they've experienced everything legal by age thirteen, why wouldn't they make inappropriate choices?

In this day and age, it takes a special kind of courage to keep kids young and wondrous, childlike, if you will. But *our* childhoods were often relaxed, and we should fight to provide our kids the identical luxury. Allow your child the joy of free time—to dream, explore, or just relax. Encourage her to develop friends in the neighborhood instead of counting on you to arrange all her social activities.

And be on the lookout for friends and neighbors who share your viewpoint. Support one another. Often other people feel just like you do. It's just that they are afraid to be the first to speak.

Occasionally, your child may even complain that she isn't involved in as many activities as some of her friends. Don't be defensive. Speak from your heart. Explain your priorities. Let her know that childhood doesn't *have* to be a time of excessive structure. Recall some of the marvelous afternoons of your youth spent at leisure as you learned more about your world and, inevitably, yourself.

Former tennis star John Evert sums it up best. He recalls his father giving the family tennis lessons in a public park. "When you couldn't get a court, you went over and played baseball or backgammon or something with friends. It was a little simpler for us. And a little more fun. But kids today, and their parents, are on a different schedule."

FRED G. GOSMAN

## Points to Remember

- Today's late bloomer is tomorrow's superstar.

- The more we force an activity on our child, the more she will hate it.

- Children allowed to develop at their own speed will usually win the race of life.

- Simply because you were overprogrammed doesn't mean your children have to be.

- If your instincts tell you your child isn't ready for an activity, he probably isn't.

- A two-year-old afforded *every* educational opportunity will be a bored first grader.

- A stress-free child is rarely success-free.

# Make It Apparent That
# You're the Parent

AVE YOU NOTICED THE RECENT SUBTLE changes in the relationships between parents and children?

The seven-year-old says to her playmate, "Let me introduce you to my friend," and points to *you*. You ask your daughter to set the table and she says, "Speak to my agent!" And your teenage son forbids you from attending the closing session of your empowerment workshop.

What is going on? When did we surrender?

Used to be, parents said, kids did. We were authority figures. You know, authority figures.

Like our ministers, and rabbis, and teachers used to be.

We were listened to. Deferred to. It was our way or no way. No longer. The mortgage is still in our name but, increasingly, the house is theirs. One diaper, one vote.

Truly democratic parents even try to be friends with their children. Isn't that a contradiction in terms? Like a flattering passport photo or a breakfast burrito? Sure, we want to be *friendly* with our kids. Tell jokes. Communicate easily. Enjoy each other's company. Share sadness. But friendship?

Look back on our own childhood. Did any of us want to be *friends* with our parents? Yuck; it's like kissing a sister. So why would our kids want to be friends with us?

Children need models of what adults should be. A recent ad for the Chevy S-10 Blazer urged parents to buy the vehicle to "show your kids you're cooler than they think." Ridiculous. We should act our age. A child would hate it if his father shouted to him to turn *up* the stereo. Can you imagine a child surprising her friends by showing up with Daddy to hear the latest toilet rocker? "Moonbeam, Stuff-Face, and Crazed, this is my father, Reginald. He's into Coke, the Diet kind. Groovy, huh?"

We're meant to be nerds, to be a tad embarrassing. It's natural law. How will kids feel cool if we're not squares?

Every child has stories he wouldn't relate to a parent, and frankly, we appreciate the silence. He'd tell a good friend. And how can you discipline a friend? Friends don't ground or deny driving privileges to one another. Friends are people you complain to about your parents. They are the ones you repay when you borrow money. They are the ones whose parents you covet.

Previously, parents could just tell it like it was! "It's bedtime." Enough said. Now we feel we need to reason with our children, make sure they understand fully the rationale for our action so they don't think us dictatorial. A mom trying to put a toddler down for the night faces a tricky situation indeed:

"Jason, it's eight o'clock. Bedtime. 'Night, 'night, honey."

Guess what? Jason has a different vision. So he asks, "*Why?*" very slowly. You know the kind of *why*? The one that takes a minute and a half from start to finish.

Heaven forbid we say, "Because I said so." So we explain. "Because you have nursery school tomorrow. You want to do well in school, don't you?"

"I hate school," Jason wails. "I hate my teacher. Why do I have to go?"

The time starts slipping away.

"Because you want to get a good education, don't you?"

"Why?"

You get the picture. Jason is just stalling, yet we fall for it all the time. All in the interest of democracy. The debate goes on so long that *we* ask for the glass of water. By the time we're done, it's ten forty-five and we're completely exhausted. In fact, we'd have been sleeping for hours if Jason hadn't nudged us twice when we began to nod off.

Some of us have moved beyond reasoning with our children, and we actually *negotiate*. Isn't that usually done between equals? We are told to rid ourselves of the outdated notion that someone wins and someone loses. If we play our cards right, our home will practically reek of consensus.

We've gone from the breakfast table to the bargaining table. Forget Dr. Spock; study Donald Trump.

Let's say we want our child to start taking out the garbage. We can't just come out and require it. That would be dictatorial. We must work a trade, negotiate. Scratch his back so he'll scratch ours. He'll take out the garbage, but we will have to offer something in exchange, like a later curfew or a new phone line.

And what do we do if our child doesn't keep up his end of the bargain? Give him heck? Forget it. *Renegotiate.*

It's funny how we behave so differently on the job. There, we are decisive. Quick-thinking. We brook no interference. We are able to successfully confront *any* challenge.

So, tell me, why can't the same person get his three-year-old daughter to obey?

If a crisis arose at work while Johnson was at home with his daughter, the conversation would probably go something like this:

"Erin, please clean your room," Daddy says. He hollers into the phone. "Smith, this is

Johnson. Something has come up, and I need that report on my desk at seven A.M. tomorrow morning."

"I can't clean up my room now, Daddy," Erin says. "I want to watch TV."

"Okay, little love," Dad says, returning four children's books to their shelves. "I know you like TV." Into the phone he says, "Smith, I don't care if you have plans tonight. Cancel them. I need the report *without fail.*"

"Daddy, can we go to the park?"

"Of course we can, sweetie," Dad says, turning off the TV and hanging two dresses over doorknobs. Meanwhile, to poor Smith: "I don't care if you have tickets to the ballet. I *need* that report. You must learn to stay on task!"

See what I mean? We can hold employees responsible but increasingly have trouble with our kids. On the job, we're managers. At home, we're Milquetoasts.

We *used* to be able to say *no*. Scary little word this *no*. Just two letters, but we sure have trouble with it. So we make excuses:

Maybe.
We'll see.

This is not a good time.
I'm too tired to decide.
I can't think about this right now.
Ask me later.
I'm busy.

Sometimes we are panicked into complete drivel. "I'll talk to your father about it," we respond, temporarily forgetting we are single mothers. "Your brother never did this!" we invoke as we passionately address our only child.

The T-shirt manufacturers have rallied to get *no* into our closets. "Because I said so." "Because I'm the mom." "What part of *no* don't you understand?" Now, if we could just get it into our heads!

We assume others will be put off by our consistency, but more likely they'll be impressed. An Ohio mom stuck to her guns and denied her hysterical three-year-old a package of gum at the grocery-store checkout. The clerk instantly complimented her for "not giving in," and told her how refreshing it was to see a mom say no and mean it.

The funny thing is, while we often berate ourselves about making decisions our children may not like, we all agree that kids prefer limits. Certainly, one East Coast child does. One day his mother found him standing in the corner. She asked, "Why?" The child responded, "I did something wrong, so I put myself in time-out."

An eight-year-old in New York was watching TV with his dad, and the father asked if the child thought he was a good daddy. The child said yes. When the father asked what made him a good father, the child responded, "Because you set rules."

Kids know that parents without rules are parents who don't care. It feels good to have parents in control. It provides a feeling of security. Perhaps ongoing misbehavior is a silent plea for parents to take charge.

Kids won't come out and *thank you* each and every time you make a decision they aren't totally fond of. One child told his mother, "No one else's mom is as mean as you are." The child's friend overheard the remark and immediately chimed in, "Oh yes, my mom is, and I always say the same thing." But in their hearts kids know you're doing your job, just like they are doing their job by arguing.

Occasionally, you read of those who benefited greatly from parental responsibility—an athlete who was denied participation in his sport for a semester due to poor grades and who subsequently excelled academically or a child from a rough neighborhood whose parents required excellence despite the odds. We always admire these families who loved their kids enough to insist on appropriate behavior. So why be so tough on ourselves? Children today are in desperate need of *limits* as well as love. They want to know that someone cares enough to make unpopular decisions.

A twelve-year-old boy perhaps best summarizes what it is kids need. Unbeknownst to his mom, he entered an essay contest sponsored by the local Catholic paper. Fifty words on "My Mom Is the Best Mom Because . . ." Know what he wrote? "My mom is the best not because of what she lets me do but because of what she *doesn't* let me do."

Will there be rewards for our daring to care? You bet! A mom in Ohio told a college sophomore he couldn't take the car back to campus because of poor grades. They raced for the car. Mom got there first and refused to get out, even when the child threatened to call the police. Eventually, the child gave up his keys, refusing to drive back to campus with a "madwoman," and didn't speak to his mom for four months.

But this past Mother's Day, the mom received a dozen roses from her son, now twenty-two and a first-year law student. The card was signed, "To the best mom, for the past twenty-two years." She cried for hours.

The good Dr. Spock has written, "Inability to be firm is the commonest problem of parents in America today." So let's level with the kids. Let them know that experience can be a wise teacher. That homes aren't democracies. That we're not their friends. That we're not as dumb as we look, and that every decision doesn't invite debate.

We parents freely admit we don't have all the answers. We should inform our children that they don't, either.

## Points to Remember

- A child who has never fantasized about having other parents is seriously lacking in imagination.

- You can't negotiate with someone who has no interest in being reasonable.

- Setting a limit isn't an invitation to debate.

HOW TO BE A HAPPY PARENT

- Children who insist on the last word are in danger of receiving a run-on sentence.

- A parent who has never embarrassed his child is probably not acting his age.

- A child with no limits is a child who will grow to hate freedom.

# Barbie Shouldn't Live Better Than We Do

P ARENTS ALL OVER THE COUNTRY ARE INCREAS-
ingly upset with rampant "gimme-itis." The economy is getting tougher and tougher, yet our kids
act as if we're made of Play-Doh. Sure, we all
secretly prayed for gifted children, but *this* is ridiculous.

Doubt and introspection confront us all. What's
best for my child? What do young ones really
need? How do we balance needs and wants? Why
didn't I invest in Crayola?

We *expect* our kids to be materialistic. An Ohio
woman returned from a Hawaii vacation and was
startled when her daughter asked, "How was

your trip?" She had expected the far more traditional, "What did you bring me?"

In California a three-year-old was asked what she wanted to be when she grew up. Know what she answered? "A customer."

Barbie is everywhere, isn't she? What an empire. Used to be, you could buy a Barbie or two and be home-free. Now there is Barbie *everything*. And have you noticed all the vehicles? The Fun Rider. The Dune Rider. The Western Motor Home. The Eastern Motor Home. My personal favorite is the Island Hopper Action Scooter (*one* island isn't good enough for Barbie). I love Barbie, but for goodness' sake, can't the girl ever walk? Why don't we just simplify our lives and have our paychecks made out directly to Mattel?

Now all the various *sequels* drive us crazy. It isn't enough to buy your son every vehicle from *Batman*. He "needs" an updated fleet when *Batman 2* is released. Holy cash registers. Who's Robin Who? We buy action figure after action figure, even though someone in his class will *always* have more.

Taking a child to the toy store is the nearest

thing to a death wish parents can have. "I want that," the child screams, forty-four *separate* times by the end of the first aisle. If this tack is unsuccessful, the kid invokes peer pressure. "Everybody in school has this. You don't want me to be left out, do you?" Next, expect a promise he has no plans to keep. "I'll be good the rest of my life! I'll never blow out another candle with my nose!" Tears come next, the out-of-control kind that instantly stop if you give in. If you still are saying no, be prepared for three tantrums, two "I don't love you"s, and one threat to call the head of the local child welfare agency.

How do we defend ourselves from this onslaught? How do we keep treats rare so that our children appreciate what they have?

I love the approach of an Indiana family. Right from the beginning, outings are either "Looking Trips" or "Shopping Trips." If a young child asks for something and the parents don't want to buy it, they firmly say, "Sorry, honey, this is a Looking Trip."

In a Southern California neighborhood, the children are urged to trade or borrow toys amongst themselves. One mom volunteers to be the bookkeeper, and all toys have a "due date." The kids actually *look forward* to trading day.

Advertising, of course, is everywhere. A New Jersey four-year-old heard a commercial with catchy music and screamed, "I want that." Turns out the commercial was for training pants, and the girl was already potty-trained!

An Illinois couple started early to educate the kids on the influence of TV commercials. Every Saturday for a month the family watched cartoons together. The girls each had a scratch pad, divided into two sections, headed "Needs" and "Wants." The advertised products had to be placed in their appropriate category. Cereals were needs; dolls were wants. One day one of the girls came running downstairs, "Look, Mommy, they are advertising a 'want' and trying to trick us into believing we 'need' it."

A Virginia mom had two kids who asked for *everything* they saw advertised on TV. She created a great system. When the kids asked for something, she wrote it down on an index card, which was put away until the following Saturday. If the children could remember what they had asked for the prior week, purchase was possible. But guess what? The kids were *never* able to remember the item they had asked for just seven days earlier!

One California couple stands up and hollers, *"We want that,"* every time an *adult* product is advertised on TV. The kids tell them they are "acting crazy." Mom and Dad readily agree.

A Texas father *anticipates* requests for toys at the Kmart, and diffuses the subject right at the entrance. "Let's look for toys we can add to your birthday list!" The child eagerly assaults the toy department, even though he'll leave empty-handed. One Iowa couple never buys their children the little nonsense items they beg for but instead credits them two dollars every time they "resist" temptation. When the child has amassed twenty dollars, he is free to select something more long-lasting. A Wisconsin family has the children donate one toy to the Salvation Army for every new one acquired.

An Illinois father had a son who had to have *everything*, so he adopted this system. He placed on the refrigerator a list with the phone numbers of six local toy stores. The child could still ask for as much as he wanted, but when he asked, the *child* had to call the six toy stores to find out if the toy was in stock and what it cost. Guess what? Requests for toys plummeted by 90 percent!

Giving children responsibility for their purchase is a wonderful idea. A New Hampshire family puts all decisions like this on their kids' backs. Each child receives exactly four poker chips at the beginning of the year, to be used at any time for spur-of-the-moment purchases worth up to twenty dollars. She can use them all in January or save them up for the coming November.

Let's remember wish lists. Just the act of adding something to a wish list enables a child to feel closer to it. And inevitably the child will change his mind and cross something off his list. What a great chance for us to say, "It's a good thing we didn't rush out to buy that truck!"

Remember, we don't always have to be "fair" every minute of our life. One Florida father of three fell into this trap. He'd find something perfect for one son, but would come home with presents for his other children as well. Till a recent Christmas. "We bought a family computer and allowed our oldest [age twelve] to open it. He said, 'Terrific, but where are the other two?' "

If I find a book for my son Bob, I buy it. A baseball card for Mike, I get it. The boys know that in the long run they receive a lot more, since if I had to *always* find a second gift, I would buy less.

Let's remember that a crisis needn't follow every time our child doesn't get his way. A youngster in Washington, D.C., asked his dad if he could have $150 for half a stretch limo for the prom. Dad said, "Heck no. I'm paying college tuition next year." Did the child run away from home? Do drugs? Nope. He looked at his dad and said, "Just thought I'd ask." Nothing wrong with asking. Nothing wrong with saying no.

Or perhaps we could work a trade. We'll pay for half the stretch limo; he'll pay for half of Harvard!

It's okay to let the kids know that *we* don't have everything, either. A Georgia mom has a pat response when one of her kids asks when he will get something terribly expensive: "When I get my mink coat and my vacation to Hawaii." Ogle the Mercedes at the stoplight. Fantasize about life in the mansion you drive by. Too often we allow our kids to think they are the only ones who don't have it all.

And remind children how long Mom and Dad have to work in order to pay for something. Often the children will conclude that it isn't worth it. A three-year-old asked for lots of toys. Mom indicated that to get them, Dad would have to work hours and hours of overtime and thus would have less time to play. The mom writes, "So far, at least, Daddy is winning."

Let's try to get away from this commercial hoopla. Give ourselves credit for many of the wonderful things we do day in and day out. Get your daughter her own phone line, but let that be the birthday present. Likewise with the expensive tennis shoes. If you're planning a trip to the zoo near your daughter's birthday, why can't it be a part of her birthday present?

My son Bob's birthday present for the last thirteen years has been tickets to Wisconsin Badger football games: lots of great memories. Caring parents do so many wonderful things with their kids; it is only a positive to count a few of them as presents. It stresses what's important—time spent with loved ones.

Time, not toys, is what our kids need. Look at

all the wonderful things we can do that are free. Go fishing. Play Frisbee. Swing in the park. Play hide-and-seek. Barbecue. These, not the plastic, are the things our kids will remember.

For this reason, don't be overconcerned if a former spouse plays "Santa Claus" to your kids. Children are very smart and realize who is paying dues and who is not. Continue to give them your love and time, and you have nothing to worry about.

An Illinois mom delights her four- and five-year-old with "hugging." The family spends hours in a local toy store, making up stories about all the different stuffed animals and giving each one a big hug.

A Florida mom writes wistfully about her "toy store," a discarded washing machine box. "All those possibilities—old clothes, hats, jewelry, feathers, foam, whatever. My friends and I created such costumes. They were original, and friends came for help and ideas." Oh yes, it was the most popular home on the block.

Stop at an occasional rummage sale. Kids can get what they want, and the prices are low. And they can see firsthand how rapidly toys depreciate. It's funny about rummage sales, isn't it? We buy a toy for $19.99, and are *happy* two years later when we sell it for fifty cents.

I had a sad experience at a recent rummage sale. An old play stove and refrigerator were for sale. Clearly, they had seen better days. The refrigerator door was slightly off its hinges. The stove was dirty and a tad wobbly. No modern conveniences were apparent—no microwave, kitchen timer, cordless phone. The burners didn't even turn red. But what amazed me was the price. This old set could be bought for just one dollar. Yet there it stood, scorned and unsold.

I began to comment to the lady in charge how sad it was that such a wonderful plaything, which must have given children countless hours of joy, could only be sold for a dollar. She mistook my comment for bargaining, and said, "You can have the pair for fifty cents."

Think of it, just fifty cents for the *pair*. How far does that go at the local toy store?

Of course, you should surprise your child with an occasional purchase. But simply because we have the money doesn't mean an item *must* be bought.

A wealthy man lived in Beverly Hills with a daughter who had to have it all. Dad was growing increasingly tired of this situation. One day they were out driving in the convertible on Rodeo Drive and the daughter saw a bike in a store window. Well, she went ballistic. Begging. Pleading. Screaming. All to no avail.

In her frustration, she suddenly shouted to her father, "Why can't I have the bike? We're rich."

Dad continued driving for a time while he collected his thoughts. Then he slowly pulled the car over to the curb, lovingly put his arm around his beautiful daughter, and said, *"We're* not rich. *I'm* rich!"

By keeping treats rare, we can give our children one of the greatest gifts of all—the thrill that comes with receiving one.

## POINTS TO REMEMBER

- Twelve action figures only excite a child until his friend has fifteen.

- The IRS should allow parents of young girls to claim Barbie as an additional dependent on their income tax return.

- Never miss an opportunity to inform a child of what *you* don't own.

- Not counting family activities as presents is the surest way to undermine their value.

- If plastic could produce happiness, psychologists wouldn't be as busy.

- They shouldn't call it Toys "Я" Us. They should call it "Torture Us."

# Say What You'll Do;
# Do What You Say

I HAVE A RATHER UNSEEMLY CONFESSION.

It embarrasses me. Worries me. Concerns me. Here it is: I don't think it is difficult to discipline effectively.

Oh, I know this is apostasy. A loving parent is to analyze an individual disciplinary challenge for weeks. Every psychological nuance of a child's misbehavior is to be plumbed, combed, delved, and plucked. Our eventual response is to reflect the insight of a Freud, the wisdom of a Solomon, the subtlety of a Picasso, and the humanity of Mother Teresa.

I'm not that smart! I'm just a C.F.R.H.!

What is the big deal? If a child misbehaves,

simply warn him of a reasonable consequence and follow through if he elects to misbehave.

That's it. No complex formulas. No nasty nuances. No hysteria. Just credibility. Consistency.

The whole key is to *warn* your child ahead of time of what will happen. We have a *plan*. No need to respond with emotion or hysteria if the misbehavior persists; just follow through. Nor should we feel *guilt*. We gave our child a choice. He was the one who elected to misbehave.

It's funny that we often feel bad about giving out a minor consequence when it is the *other* stuff that hurts—the words: "What kind of a girl are you?" "How could you be so stupid?" "How can you be such an ingrate?" "Is this the appreciation I get?"

And the scene: We start yelling; the child starts yelling. Before you know it, we've both said things we can never retract. How much better simply to follow through.

Too often we are ineffective, hesitating to mete out a consequence that will matter. A four-year-old Texas girl bit her six-year-old brother on the ear. Mom said that if it ever recurred, the daughter would spend one *hour* in her room. She looked at Mom, looked at her brother, and said, "Cheap enough,'' bit him again, and walked to her room.

We need to give our kids a TARTAR.

You heard me, a TARTAR.

What's that? Not tartar sauce. That's for fish. Just a plain old TARTAR.

Remember the Tartars? The aggressive people from the steppes of Russia who conquered their neighbors. Okay, not the greatest role models, but give a TARTAR anyway. So I'm not good with acronyms. Sue.

A TARTAR—a Timely, Appropriate Response They'll Always Remember.

That's all it takes. Follow through. Once. Maybe twice. And when our kids see we are serious, much of our problem will be over.

A Midwestern mom gave her daughter a TARTAR. They had gone to a variety store, and the daughter just had to have *everything*—a coloring book, new crayons, gum, candy, you name it. Mom was put off, and finally allowed her daughter just to buy a Coke.

When they returned home, the daughter was still in a huff. She wouldn't leave the car, and demanded that her mother drive her back to the store. As it happened, the girl's father was mowing the lawn, and it was a very hot day. So the mother grabbed the unopened Coke from her daughter and said, "Daddy, look what your thoughtful daughter was kind enough to bring you from the store!" (She describes the look on her daughter's face as "priceless.")

A New Jersey mother had a problem with her two children, ages three and six, taking baths. After "months" of hollering and complaining, the mother informed the kids of a simple rule. If they weren't in the tub two minutes after being called, then they would go to bed without bath *and* stories. "One night of bed without stories and now they run when called."

An Illinois father was confronting several misbehaving children in church. Get hysterical? Ignore the problem? Not a chance. He told them that if they continued to misbehave, they would stay for the *next mass.*" Which they did. "Now," the father writes, "my children don't talk, and fellow parishioners compliment me on how well behaved they are."

A Kentucky mother was standing in line at Wendy's with a misbehaving child. She warned, "If you continue, I'll take you home." The child persisted and was soon dining on peanut butter and jelly. As the mom says, "He was disap-

pointed, but it was a long time before he misbehaved in line again."

A California father found himself with a daughter who was "allergic" to homework. After
months of crises, he simply said, "From now on,
every time your teacher tells me you didn't turn
in an assignment, your telephone will be taken
from your room for three days." After he followed through just once, "the allergy disappeared."

If we are confronted with really serious misbehavior, like failure to do homework or swearing
*at* us, we shouldn't hesitate to invoke the biggies,
like missing a soccer game or a school dance.
"How can I deny my child these things? He loves
them." That's the idea. If he knows we'll follow
through, he can elect to change his behavior, so
that in fact *nothing* will have to be denied.

Consistency and follow-through are especially
needed if the children are going through a crisis,
like divorce or the death of a parent. Of course
you should be sensitive, talk about feelings, and
obtain counseling if needed. But if your children
know that they are *still* responsible for their misbehavior, they will more likely remain on track
during these difficult periods.

HOW TO BE A HAPPY PARENT

Likewise if you have only visitation rights and have your children for just a short time. It is so tempting to ignore misbehavior. We don't want to ruin the weekend. But we *must* invest in discipline so that future outings will be joyful.

Sometimes we have to go the extra mile to be *able* to follow through. An eighth grader in Colorado begged her parents to allow her to go on the class trip to Washington. The parents put down a hefty deposit but informed their daughter that she wouldn't be allowed to go if she had academic or behavior problems. The daughter confidently said, "You'll let me go. Otherwise, you'll lose your deposit." So on-the-spot Mom wrote out a separate check for trip-cancellation insurance. The daughter "has toed the line ever since."

If you are willing to inconvenience yourself in the name of discipline, the battle is half over. Leave Grandma's early if the children are acting impossible. Depart the ballpark in the sixth inning if you've warned the kids and their behavior is still poor. If we do something like this *once,* our kids will remember it for a long time.

We can learn plenty from our children, too. A Colorado mom discovered the importance of

FRED G. GOSMAN

follow-through when her teenage daughter baby-sat her son. "How'd it go?" Mom asked upon returning. "Okay," the daughter replied. "He misbehaved, and I had to send him to his room." "How'd you get him to go?" Mom asked. The daughter responded, "Mom, I'm not like you. When I say something, I mean it."

I dearly love to see my kids use my techniques on me. Mike especially does this. Perhaps I've promised him I'd drive him to a friend's, yet I fall asleep on the couch. Mike will approach and utter something especially sensitive, like, "If you're not up by the count of five, I'll sit on you." Sheep-ishly, I beg him not to be "punitive," to no avail. Once I learned he followed through, I became quite adept at rising swiftly.

Children will communicate our rules to their younger siblings, so our job is made simpler. A mom had a foster child in her home. She told him that he would never be hit but that if he misbe-haved, something would be taken away. Her own son piped in, "You better believe her, too, be-cause she'll do it."

Appropriate behavior can become such a part of our home that we can even be in shock if our child elects to call our bluff. One father sternly counts to three when his kids are misbehaving, and since the children know he means business, they change their behavior. But one day the six-year-old didn't. Dad got to "three" and had no idea what to do. "In five years, everyone always complied. I felt like a jerk."

What if you impose a reasonable consequence and your child doesn't cooperate? Simple. Raise the ante. You had given a time-out, and yet your child is still carrying on, making a mockery of it. Don't get emotional. Simply give another choice. "If you continue to talk, we won't go to the park to swing after dinner. You decide what you would like. I can live with whatever you choose." And then simply follow through if your child elects to test you.

If we discipline effectively when the child is young, we can, hopefully, avoid a lot of problems later. Sure, a six-month-old baby is an innocent. But most parents agree that by age two or three, children can be held responsible for some of their actions. Too often we ignore the misbehavior, hoping against hope it will go away.

Will a TARTAR make us feel good? Not always.

The kids will often work us over pretty good. But so what? The purpose of discipline is not for us to feel good. It's to create beneficial change with our kids.

A mom who sent her five-year-old daughter to her room found a cutely misspelled note slipped under her door: "Ples lat me out." She kept the note for posterity but kept her daughter in the room for the duration.

A mother adopted a rule that if her daughter wanted a homemade lunch, she had to tell her the night before. Otherwise, she would eat at school. "The first time she forgot, I sent a sobbing seven-year-old off to school, and I felt like a horrible mother. But she hasn't forgotten since."

Kids sometimes try to embarrass us. A mom was stuck in a *long* grocery line with a misbehaving son. She said, "One more time, and you'll have a time-out when you get home." The child suddenly started shouting, "Mommy, please don't be angry with me. You're not going to hit me *again,* are you?"

A three-year-old who had moved into a new neighborhood had to spend a few minutes in her room as a time-out. She rolled down the windows

HOW TO BE A HAPPY PARENT

and screamed, "My parents don't love me. They locked me in my room. Will somebody help me escape?" The parents persisted, but the neighbors still laugh about it!

Threats to call in the authorities are not uncommon. In one house, it doesn't matter what the consequence is. It is never "legal," even if it's just not being allowed to watch television. Two Michigan boys routinely threatened to call the child-welfare authorities. Then their mother taped the number to their phone. Hasn't heard this threat since.

Kids will play up to our guilt. In Massachusetts, a child was refusing to take a bath. So Mom gave him a choice. "If you don't take the bath, you can't watch *Rudolph the Red-Nosed Reindeer* on television tonight and will have to go to bed." The child chose bed.

A few minutes later he came out of his room and asked his mom, "Do you feel bad?" Mom cracked up and asked the child to repeat the question. "Do you feel bad that you put me to bed?" Mom said, "No, I don't." To which the child said, "I'm ready for my bath now."

Be prepared for the occasional "I don't

love you" from a child who elects not to change his behavior. Simply respond, "Well, I love you," and change the subject. The more we ignore these very hurtful words, the less we will hear them.

Discipline is *not* a full-time job. What is full-time is the yelling and screaming and threatening. All we have to do is follow through once or twice, and the child will realize it is best to quit testing us. We can enjoy our children more, as good times will not be ruined by misbehavior.

Sometimes we secretly admire the behavior of *other* kids. "If only ours were like that," we say. Perhaps they could be if we disciplined like *their* parents.

Do yourself a favor. Pick a reasonable consequence for the one or two behaviors you would most like to change in your kids, and then just follow through. Without emotion. Without guilt. Calmly, confidently, and surely.

*Say what you'll do; do what you say.* It sounds simple. It can be simple.

And it will give us greater calm in our homes if we but have the resolve to do it.

HOW TO BE A HAPPY PARENT

## Points to Remember

- Don't give threats; give promises.

- If misbehavior lasts twenty years, it's more than a stage.

- If we survived *our* parents, our children will probably survive us.

- The less concerned a parent is with being popular, the more popular he'll be.

- The more reasonable the consequence, the greater the cooperation.

- A parent who never disciplines will have a child unsure of his parents' love.

- When you discipline effectively, you rarely need to discipline.

# Money Doesn't Grow on Cash Machines

ALTHOUGH OUR CHILDREN TEND TO *SPEND* lots of money, that doesn't mean they *know* much about it.

In Colorado, a five-year-old girl was presented with a dollar for her first allowance. She stared at the picture on the currency. "Is his name Bill?" she asked. "No," Mom replied. "That's George Washington, our first president. What made you think it was Bill?" "You know," her daughter replied. "Dollar bill."

A Long Island three-year-old received a dollar in a birthday card. She was disappointed. Said the girl, "Mom, I have it already." An Ohio six-year-

HOW TO BE A HAPPY PARENT

old celebrated his sixth birthday by asking Mom and Dad for his own Visa card!

All the changes in technology confound many adults; *think* of what they do to our kids. Take cash machines. A mom was shopping with her daughter, who asked for a toy. "I don't have the money," mom replied. "No problem," the child said. "Just go to that machine and get some!"

Have you ever thought how mind-boggling these machines must be to young kids? When we buy them gum balls, they *see* a penny or nickel go into the machine before their gum comes out. Not so here. Do you think our kids realize that our account is being instantly debited at our financial institution? Or do they know what truly happens when we write a check?

In a New Jersey home, a child is convinced the long number on her mom's cash machine card is really the *balance* in the account. And in Ohio, a youngster has sage advice for Mom when the machine inquires if another transaction is desired: "Say *yes*, Mom. You'll get *more money*!"

A quick-thinking Texas child had a harsh introduction to the realities of our credit economy. He regularly bought lunch at grade school with money his parents supplied. One day Dad noticed how much money his son had saved and complimented him. The next day, a bill came from school, for ten dollars, for lunches. The father asked his son what was up. He responded proudly, "The other day in lunch line, the kid in front of me said, 'Charge it,' and didn't have to pay. So I figured the money was better off with me."

Let's educate our kids about money. Have them keep a simple budget. Fifty cents a day at school for a candy bar doesn't sound like much. But it's a *hundred dollars* a year.

Once they are given limits, children will be much smarter consumers. A dad took his three kids to Walt Disney World and was sure they would ask for tons of treats. So he gave them fifty dollars apiece and allowed them to keep whatever was left. The nine-year-old spent twelve dollars. The twelve-year-old spent eighteen, and the fourteen-year-old spent it all but didn't ask for any more. And the dad is convinced he saved *hundreds* of dollars.

Kids *can* budget. A very wise mom in St. Louis was tired of her eight-year-old son always complaining about the birthday party she had worked so hard to arrange. So she put her son in charge. It was *his* responsibility to call around, to find out the costs of the different birthday packages. The child received a specific budget and worked hard to arrange a party where every available cent was spent.

He selected a bowling-and-pizza party. At the pizza parlor, the birthday boy was seated at the head of the table, and for some reason his best friend was down at the other end. Suddenly, the birthday boy heard his friend inappropriately ask the waitress, "May I have extra cheese on my pizza?" The birthday boy rose from his chair, raced to the other end of the table, and told his friend, *"No you can't. That's too expensive!"*

Kids must learn about the financial world around them. If they are old enough, have them help balance the bank statement. If you own property, put a youngster in charge of recording rental income and all your expenses; perhaps he'll have a future in real estate. If your child has to file an income tax return, be sure to have her help if she is old enough to do so.

Let's begin to teach our kids that our financial pie has limits, that more money spent on them causes shortages elsewhere. A child was at a toy store and asked for a toy. Mom said, "Sorry, the electric bill was too big last month." For the next thirty days, that child went around the house turning off the lights!

Rather than just saying no to a child's request, perhaps respond, "Sorry, it's not in the budget." Let him know you are working with limited resources. Or perhaps say, "We can get it, but what should we cut back on? Movies? Bowling? Pizza?"

If times get tough, don't scare your child, but communicate the need to save money. A very wise Florida dad challenged his family. He said that if six thousand dollars could be saved, one thousand of that could be used on a summer vacation. Every family member pitched in and tried to think of additional ways to save. They met their goal and had the vacation of their dreams.

I'm often asked when children should start to get an allowance. Most parents begin in the five-to-eight age range. But the important question is, When do you want to begin teaching money management?

I love the approach of one Ohio family. Mom would put a number of different coins in front of the kids, and they could select four. She made sure that the pennies were always shined up.

When the children started selecting the dirty old quarters rather than the glistening pennies, Mom knew it was time to start giving an allowance.

I have some unusual ideas about allowances. First, I think allowances should be *bigger*, with a clear listing of what responsibilities are the child's. Toys? School lunches? Gum at the grocery store? Video rentals? Athletic fees? Treats at movies? Gifts for friends' birthdays and for coaches? Miniature golf? It wouldn't necessarily *cost* us more, but it would encourage our children to spend responsibly.

But I have one more radical idea. If you can afford to do so, pay your child thirteen weeks of allowance at a time. My children are both teenagers, and I am here to say that it works wonderfully. I *beg* you to try it.

It really simplifies your life. I just circle January 1, April 1, July 1, and October 1 on my calendar. I avoid the weekly hassle of distributing the allowances. I never have the correct change, and inevitably the kids claim you owe them for the last half century.

Does giving out so much money at once entail a risk? You bet. Perhaps the child will decide to spend it all at once. But I ask you, would that be the worst thing? If we refuse to bail him out in the tenth or twelfth week, wouldn't that be one of the best lessons our child could ever have? If your children are younger, and thirteen weeks seems like a lifetime, perhaps circle the first of every month, and disburse as many weeks' allowance as there are Sundays in the month.

We should encourage our children to save. Many parents take their children to the bank every week to make a deposit. Some even drive Grandma three miles out of the way so she can see "Emily's bank." A four-year-old in Connecticut learned saving early and now prefers putting his money in his Coke bottle bank rather than buying gum balls or candy. "We just started talking about what to do with *his* money."

Often, children are required to save half their birthday, Christmas, or baby-sitting money. One Michigan family gives an allowance every ten weeks, but if the child can't produce half of that as savings at the end of the period, he misses a month's allowance. Some families offer "premium" interest to attract young savers, while others *match* interest earned on savings. A New Jersey family assesses 10 percent "taxes and So-

cial Security" on all money the child earns or receives and returns it, with interest, at age
eighteen.

Have your child pay you back if she borrows
money from you. Don't, out of kindness, forget
about it. And sometimes, ask *her* for money.
Works wonders.

When the child pays part of the cost, or the
whole cost, he will respond like a consumer and
care how his money is spent. A child was at a
mall with his mom and wanted cheese balls and
a Coke. Mom said the child would have to pay.
When he learned the cost was $3.50, he said, "No
way."

A mother was at Toys "Я" Us with a child who
was driving her crazy. The child just *had* to buy
something. Finally, frustrated, she gave her son
ten dollars to buy whatever he wanted. The child
looked and looked, all to no avail. Finally, he announced there was "nothing he wanted to buy
with *his* ten dollars."

A child in Connecticut won a scholarship to
space camp. The next summer, he wanted to return. The parents said he would have to earn half
the money. He did. These parents swear that the
best way of knowing whether a child really wants

something is if he's prepared to use his own money.

A Colorado four-year-old has become a smart shopper by using her own money. The father reports that frequently the child thinks of buying something, but then realizes she would rather not. "She now saves for the things she really wants."

Often children cooperate, out of economic necessity. Many families relate how their kids worked *together* to save for a Nintendo or something expensive they each wanted. And enterprise is spurred. A child who wanted to switch from a Nintendo system to Genesis sold the unit and all his cartridges to a friend and only had to come up with twenty dollars of his own.

Kids love to participate. It makes them feel good. A Kentucky father built a birdhouse with his daughter. He asked her if she would be willing to chip in a small amount each month to help pay for birdseed. The daughter said, "Sure." Same with food for dogs and cats. It gives kids a good feeling.

Let's encourage the work ethic. With the number of family businesses and farms decreasing, children often don't get the early exposure to work they did previously. Nurture these young efforts, and support entrepreneurial children whenever you can.

An Illinois mom thought of an ingenious way for her six-year-old twins to earn extra money. She signed up to deliver phone books. Mom did the driving, but it was the kids who carried the phone books from the car to the front porches of neighboring homes. They got to keep all the money and have already asked Mom to please sign up for more blocks next year.

An eight-year-old in Michigan raises a crop of pumpkins to sell for extra spending money. The neighbors look forward to her coming door-to-door. An Ohio daughter earns extra money by growing vegetables to sell to neighbors. She already has purchased a Walkman and receives constant calls inquiring when her next harvest will be in.

There are lots of novel ways to get money into the hands of kids. One couple puts their son in charge of clipping coupons. His incentive? He gets to keep a quarter of what Mom saves at the grocery store. Another couple encourages their child to become really good at washing cars. He has "contracts" with half the drivers on the block. A Louisiana family has the son call competing insurance agencies to obtain quotes on policies about to be renewed. He gets to keep 50 percent of any savings and learns about insurance in the process.

Baby-sitting is a great job for youngsters. Kids now often earn three dollars an hour and up. Sit four hours, earn twelve bucks. And often the child sleeps some of the time.

Mowing lawns is a wonderful activity for male and female teenagers. If they are willing to walk behind a self-propelled mower for less than an hour on a seventy-degree day, they can earn about ten bucks. *Great pay.* Same with snow shoveling. During a recent Pittsburgh blizzard, neighborhood kids were charging ten dollars to clear a sidewalk. Said one of the female shovelers, "I hope it snows like this every year. This is fun."

Supporting your child's efforts is mandatory, but sometimes it can be a pain. My son Bob was a vendor at Milwaukee County Stadium this past summer, and of course I would buy whatever he was selling. The problem was that some of Bob's friends also vended, and I would support them, too. After a hot dog from Tim, nachos from Andy, and a Dove Bar from Chris, Bob would invariably appear and ask, "How many cotton candies are you good for?"

Bottom line, our children have to learn that gratification can be deferred. I love the playful strategy of a Georgia family. Whenever the child asks for something particularly expensive, they respond, "Maybe for your bar mitzvah." The two hundred-dollar tennis shoes? "Maybe for your bar mitzvah." The five-hundred-dollar CD player? "Wonderful. Maybe for your bar mitzvah." You might be wondering why this strategy is so darn successful, but I think you'll comprehend its effectiveness once you learn this happens to be a *Catholic* family.

A Chicago father took his six-year-old daughter on her own special date to see *The Nutcracker*. The two-year-old asked when it would be her turn to go. Mom wisely said, "When the pretty velvet dress your sister wore fits you." The youngster knew one day the dress would fit, and waited patiently until she was in first grade, just like her sister.

Can't you imagine the little girl's excitement every Christmas as she tried on that pretty velvet dress? How her heart must have been racing when it finally fit? She probably didn't sleep the night before going to *The Nutcracker.* Heck, she probably slept through *The Nutcracker.* But this is the kind of excitement we can provide our children when we leave them things to look forward to.

But let's remember that there are plenty of times for generosity. A New Jersey father had a sixteen-year-old who just *had* to have a car. He bought it for his daughter but required her to make monthly payments to him. She baby-sat and worked hard to earn the money and dearly *loved* her car. Drove it all the time while maintaining high grades. Seven years later she met the man of her dreams. On her wedding day, as her father toasted her future, he fought back tears and handed her a special envelope. In it was all the money she had paid for the car, with interest.

It had been his plan all along.

## Points to Remember

- The average child collects about three hundred weeks' allowance a year.

- The best way for a youngster to learn the value of money is for you to borrow it from him.

- Never walk past a lemonade stand without buying a cup.

- The kid next door always has a bigger allowance.

- The best way to ensure a child's future is to instill a work ethic.

- The last lawnmower a teen walked behind shouldn't have been giving off bubbles.

# Never Ground a Child for More Than Twenty Years

SIMPLY BECAUSE WE ARE BIGGER THAN OUR children doesn't mean that we should go out of our way to throw our weight around. In fact, the more reasonable we are with them, the better their behavior is likely to be.

No one appreciates a fanatic. If the kid is two minutes late for curfew, so what? Ignore it. Ask if he had a good time. If the baseball game goes into extra innings, don't walk around saying, "Bedtime is bedtime." Sit down and watch.

Flexibility is important. One family forbids swearing, except if it is part of the story. Another forbids excessive door slamming but allows "one good one," since Mom remembers how exciting that was.

Manners can be tough for kids; even adults have trouble with them. Don't harp on discipline ten times a day. We had our kids to enjoy, not to lecture.

Discipline has to be reasonable. I was in a restaurant once and a very stupid mother said to her eight-year-old daughter, "If you don't behave, I'll throw you in the washing machine when we get home."

I hope this lady will not follow through. But her daughter knows this. Mom thought she was proclaiming a severe consequence, but in practice it was no different than offering none.

Likewise for a mom who threatened physical punishment. She was saying to her son, "Dylan, if you don't stop it, I'm going to beat you," and Dylan looked up at her, smiled, and concluded, "I know. Till I don't grow anymore." Her letter to me was signed, "Empty-Threat Mom."

Ridiculous threats can become a way of life: "Tomorrow morning this television set is going to be on the front lawn!" Not likely. "If you aren't ready in three minutes, I will leave without you!"

"If you don't behave, you're going to walk *the rest of the way home!*"

Watch out for the word *never*. Using it is a sure way of knowing you are about to say something really *dumb*. "If your room isn't clean by dinnertime, you will *never* be allowed to play basketball again." "If your dollies are not put away by the count of three, I will *never* buy you another Barbie." "If you aren't home by eleven, you will *never* use the car again."

Sometimes we penalize ourselves instead of the kids. A Texas woman had two young daughters who loved to help clean. Believe it or not, they would fight over who would get to mop. One day they were really carrying on, and the mom said, "If you continue to argue, I'll do the mopping." You know the rest of the story.

The same with grounding. I've never been a big believer in it. It's too hard to monitor. Rarely does the child serve his full term. And we have to run our own errands!

One mom grounded her son for an entire *semester* for poor grades. She will *never forget* this punishment. Having him around all the time was "nigh unto torture." She now reminds her grown children to keep their punishments realistic.

HOW TO BE A HAPPY PARENT

If you do find yourself having imposed something that you later feel is excessive, the answer is simple. Commute it. Admit your error.

I did this once with Bob. He had done something, and I said, "If you do it again, we won't go to the opening game of the Green Bay Packers." Pretty dumb of me. We had always gone, so it was a tradition I wasn't prepared to break. So I substituted something else, and yes, we had a great time at the game.

The more creative the consequences, the easier our task might be. I love the policy of a middle-school teacher in Chicago. When the kids have to stay after school, he makes them listen to Frank Sinatra music.

Or let's say our child is swearing and that is unacceptable. One family solved this, not through hysteria, but by getting physical. The child could swear as much as he wanted, but every time he did, he owed mom twenty-five sit-ups. After the first three days, swears were history.

Use your imagination. There's great stuff out there. A New Jersey couple starts singing loudly in a restaurant whenever their kids misbehave. A Colorado family has the teenagers collect a large trash bag full of neighborhood litter.

It's the nineties, so let's make sure our consequences are up-to-date. Used to be, sending a child to his room was okay. Not much to do there. Now, isn't that the place with all the electronic stuff? The TV, radio, CD player, Nintendo, etc. Sounds like a *reward*; amazing the kids ever come out.

If you have trouble thinking of reasonable consequences, ask the kids! Really. I never did this, but many parents allow the children to select the consequence, and routinely report that the kids select something more *severe* than what the parents would have. Isn't that ironic, and doesn't it say a lot? Here we are, scratching our heads, trying to think of a consequence that we won't feel guilty about, and on their own, kids select consequences *tougher* than we would.

Some families rely on humorous code words so children know it is time to shape up or consequences will follow. For one son, "Far-fig-nugen," another, "Hose brain." Words can be whispered in public, written in church. Not a bad idea. No need to lecture or chastise. Just utter the secret word. And let's remember to tailor our consequences to the child. For one, sports might be the answer; for another, television; for another, fines.

Don't expect the youngster to compliment you on your consequence. He will usually feign indifference. "Take away the Nintendo. I don't care." That's why we need to stick with the consequence. The first day, our child may not miss the bike or phone. By the fifth, he may well discover that cooperation is the path of least resistance.

Simply because misbehavior recurs doesn't mean "there is nothing I can do with my child." Try a different consequence. It may take a while to find the true motivator for your child, but it is certainly worth the effort.

Don't worry; you're not destroying children's independence by enforcing your standards. A New Jersey father required his child to *stand* during time-outs. The child preferred to sit. It became a constant struggle that Dad always eventually won. One day the child said, "Just so you know, I'm standing on the outside, but sitting on the inside."

Often the surest way to *avoid* misbehavior is to invite children to do it. Especially if you have a playful consequence. Let's say your son leaves dishes all over the house. Rather than getting in an uproar, why not say, "For every ten dishes you leave around the house, I get breakfast in bed." And then "root" for him to leave dishes. Say, "I can smell that bacon already," whenever you find one. *Beg* him to leave his dishes on the floor, so that you are closer to dining in your bed. The more you "encourage" their misdeeds, the more they will "spite" you by behaving.

Many people like to make consequences *natural* outgrowths of a child's actions. For example, if the child stuffs himself before mealtime, there are no desserts for three days. If your daughter hits a friend, then they can't play together for a week.

These are all okay, but I have *trouble* thinking of natural consequences. And sometimes the penalty seems contrived. One mom confronted a child who wouldn't drain the water out of the tub. So she filled all her plastic containers with the bathwater and put them in his room. When he was tired of the water being there, he had to wash and dry the containers and put them away. Cute, but lots of work for Mom. Why not say, "If you don't drain the tub, there is no television tonight."

What if a child does something serious? Like swear at a parent. Can't a dad deny his child use of a bike or baseball bat? Threaten nonattendance at the school dance or the soccer game? Take away Nintendo for a week? Deny access to the car? Unless you stretch, there is no "natural" connection between the swearing and denying him these privileges or possessions. But these can be some of the most effective consequences at our disposal.

Let's remember that, wherever possible, parents should agree on discipline. If Mom is strict and Dad is a soft touch, no one is going to be happy, especially the kid. The parents might have to compromise, but that is better than inconsistency. And remember to communicate consequences. If Mom and Dad are working different shifts, use a blackboard or bulletin board to leave messages in case new consequences have been imposed or new rewards earned.

Sometimes after a divorce, children are exposed to different rules in their parents' homes. No question that it is best for the parents to agree on discipline and support each other. But that is not always possible. Remember that children see lots of different disciplinary approaches. At school. At church. At their aunt's. At their friends'. At Grandma's. They are smart, and very adaptable. As long as you are consistent, kids should be able to conform to *your* limits.

Often our discipline will have salutary effects

beyond our imagination. A soccer coach made a team of "chatty girls" run extra laps. Team members wound up in "fantastic" shape. But here's my favorite. One couple had their misbehaving children stand in a corner for five minutes when they returned home from church. As they got older, they had to write ten sentences given by their father. "Now our twelve- and thirteen-year-olds have perfect writing. The oldest behaved and never had to write. Has *awful* writing!"

We must be reasonable with our children, we must be fair, and we must be creative. But we also must remember to be clear:

A child was with his mother at Toys "Я" Us and came across an action figure he wasn't familiar with.

"*What* the hell is this?" he asked, *loudly.*

Mom was mortified. She had raised the child in a strict manner, and she was shocked by his language. Everyone in the aisle came to a standstill as shoppers strained to gaze upon this wonder child.

Mom looked at her child and asked sternly, "What did you say?"

The child was temporarily confused. It didn't immediately occur to him what he had done wrong. He thought and thought about his last sentence. Tens of shoppers were staring at him. Mom was giving a look that would kill. And he was getting nowhere.

Suddenly, it occurred to him, and he felt immense relief. In an even louder voice, he shouted, "Pardon me. *Who* the hell is this?"

## POINTS TO REMEMBER

- Concentrate on the biggies.

- Never use the word *never*.

- If you send a misbehaving child to his room, be sure to turn off the circuit breakers.

- A child who doesn't remember her middle name or phone number can recall *every* consequence you have ever given out.

- The harder it is to enforce a consequence, the less likely you are to follow through.

- The best friend's folks are always more reasonable.

# A Child Who Can Program a VCR Is Capable of Mastering a Washer and Dryer

**D**ID YOU HEAR ABOUT THAT CASE IN MIS-souri? A father asked his son to clean the basement. The child responded, "Sorry, Dad, it's not in my job description!"

What's going on here? The child who makes the mess often winds up watching an *adult* clean it up. Working moms end their exhausting days not with reading a good book but with doing loads of laundry for their teenagers.

A Midwestern four-year-old was told by Dad to help clean up the mess she made. Soon the child was overheard muttering, "Three meals a day, a warm bed, and clean clothes ... that's what I get for *all* the work I do around here."

It's time to get some help around the house! Let's follow the example of the athletes. Increasingly, they talk trash. Let's do that with the kids: Talk some trash. And some dishes. Beds. Closets. Laundry.

The stereotype of the selfless, chore-burdened mom is still alive and well. An ad for the Fairmont Hotel brags, "The last time you had this kind of service you were probably living with your mother." The sign in the hospital's nurses' station reads, "Your mother doesn't live here. Clean up after *yourself*!"

But it's the nineties—moms need to come out of the closet, too. So many women endure such hectic schedules, frantically trying to balance their jobs with domestic responsibilities. Often, time to enjoy family is lost. But *all* moms, whether they are employed outside the home or not, need help. Deserve help.

Every so often an unappreciated mom goes on strike, and we read about it in the news. I say, Right on! If the kids are old enough, we should all take a day off. I'm picking September 9. Call it Parent Appreciation Day. Mark your calendar.

Okay, there would be a little chaos. Seventy percent of the nation's kids would show up tardy. Ninety percent would forget their homework. But we'll survive. Who knows, *broiled* peanut butter and jelly might be delicious. Maybe Gatorade works as well in the dishwasher as the Cascade.

Kids actually think we *enjoy* chores, you know. A New Jersey mom was disciplining her four-year-old. In a snit, the little boy said, "If you don't let me watch TV, I won't let you cook for me tonight!"

It's amazing what some kids do to help out around the house. Dust. Make lunches for the whole family. Strip the beds. Clean the bathrooms. Girls *and* boys. Many children don't let their parents know what their friends are required to do; they're scared to give ideas.

In Ohio, a mom requires beginning middle-schoolers to do their own laundry. In fact, during the previous summer, the child helps mom with *everyone's* laundry. By the time September comes, the child actually thinks that just doing his *own* laundry is a snap.

Make a short list of some of the required chores. It might look like this:

cooking

loading dishwasher

mowing lawn

emptying dishwasher

feeding pets

emptying waste

dusting

baskets

ironing

folding laundry

vacuuming

cleaning floors

shopping

setting table

cleaning

clearing table

doing laundry

taking out garbage

polishing silver

Would it be so bad if we assigned some of these to our kids? Sure, they're busy. But so are we.

Maybe we can prepare a chore wheel, and younger kids can spin each week to see which responsibilities will be theirs. Mike and Bob used to play a game of pool Monday night after dinner, to determine who would clear and who would load the dishwasher during the coming week. Some homes have the children "volunteer" for chores, with the youngest going first. Others give their children complete responsibility for maintaining a different common room each week.

One Missouri family has each chore written on

a slip of paper and spreads them out on the living room carpet. The children, and then the adults, select three slips. Afterward, there is a three-minute "barter" period that the kids *"love!"* They all try to negotiate the best possible deal for themselves, at the siblings', children's, or parents' expense.

Most of us complain about how much TV our children watch. Why can't they use this time to fold the laundry? Might just give them motivation to pick up a book.

A Georgia mom has "Your Night to Cook" for her six- and eight-year-old boys. With great patience, she explained the ways of the kitchen, and with *intense* supervision, the boys became comfortable and competent. They make dinner twice a week, and "love" doing it.

Chores *you* did for years will suddenly become unnecessary. The daughter who is allergic to wrinkles will come out against ironing. The eight-year-old assigned to rake leaves suddenly becomes a naturalist. Your son claims a preference for the feel of a dirty sheet.

Kids will always have ideas for making their chores easier, even if it's their first day on the job. A child who was in charge of making sure toilet paper was always in the bathrooms placed a pile of forty-two rolls next to *each* toilet. Made his job "easier!" So what if the parents thought they were "living in a Charmin commercial."

The teenager who bench-presses a truck will insist you buy a lighter vacuum cleaner. Your daughter will recommend the purchase of an institutional-size washer and dryer. And though you've suffered silently with arthritis for years, your son will try to work you over for an automatic can opener.

Beware children trying to pull the steel wool over your eyes. One day my son Mike was cleaning up after dinner. When we came home, we were surprised to see a messy broiler pan sitting on the stove. When we asked Mike about it, he responded with great confidence, "You asked me to do the *dishes!*"

Some teens might seek to be paid for helping out, and this is a no-no. One mom asked her son to do the dishes. The child responded, "Sure, for five bucks." Mom ignored the comment and did the cleaning up. But two days later the child asked to be driven to a friend's house. "Sure," Mom answered. "For five bucks."

Actually, you can *use* chores as a source of ad-

FRED G. GOSMAN

ditional money for your kids. You might have two lists. The A list has chores that the child owes the family; they are his responsibility as a family member. But the B list includes chores that the child may elect to do in return for money. Consider using chores as a consequence, also. It is a heck of a lot more helpful than merely sending a child to his room.

Some parents routinely reward their children if chores are completed on schedule. A very successful system in one home is to give a child one chore a day. If he does them all, each week he earns a small amount of money to be spent at Toys "Я" Us. Per the mother, "Since putting this system into place, he hasn't missed *one* day's responsibilities."

In Michigan, one home has a "fun box," where children throw in suggestions during the week for fun weekend activities. Mom and Dad draw an idea out of the box first thing Sunday morning *only* if chores for the week have been successfully completed.

Of course not all kids will cooperate, especially at first, as they test us. In some homes there's a "natural" consequence for not doing your chore. Forget to empty the cat litter, and the litter box

HOW TO BE A HAPPY PARENT

spends the night in your room. Children who don't change sheets find their beds stripped. Ignore the trash, and it's piled on your bed.

Getting the kids in the pocketbook has occurred to more than one parent. In one home, a child who doesn't do the dishes pays for the family's restaurant meal the following night. In another house the daughter is fined a dollar a day for not walking the dog. In one family the twins are paid twenty-five cents apiece to clean their room. But if Mom has to do it, the kids must pay Mom fifty cents. "I don't have to clean it very often!"

One mother simply does the chore that the child neglected to do. But that evening, "without fail," the child owes thirty minutes of help with *her* chores. Often, additional chores are assigned if responsibilities are not fulfilled and steps are implemented to ensure that they're done.

If kids know we are serious, their cooperation will usually follow. In Colorado, a football player was told to clean the basement. He ignored the request. On game day, he was looking for his uniform. Mom said she would wash it when the basement was clean. Quickly, he did a slap-dash job. When he was done, Mom gave him his pants. The young man asked, "Where's my top?" Mom responded, "You cleaned up halfway, you'll dress halfway!" The remaining work was completed quickly.

A Midwestern mom came home from a visit to Grandma and found the house a mess. She informed the children of her disappointment. The next day the kids cleaned their rooms and prepared a chore list for *themselves.*

Many benefits flow from children learning responsibility in the home. One mother was surprised to find that after she taught her child to make an occasional meal, complaints about *her* meals disappeared. A Florida woman was upset when her son went away to college; what she missed most were the conversations they'd had as they did the dishes together.

An Oregon mom put her child in charge of his own laundry when he was ten. Now, when she occasionally throws in his jeans with hers, she is actually *thanked.*

Children can learn to cooperate. Three teenagers were given complete responsibility for their own laundry. They communicated, and decided to alternate. Says the mom, "It's just about the only thing they agree on." In another home, a week with all the chores done earns everyone a trip to the local pizza parlor. The kids stay on top of one another and even do each other's chores. Writes the mom, "It's teamwork now."

Do we want to turn our kids into slaves? Of course not. But if we can make our boys better husbands, and all our children more responsible, while giving ourselves more free time to enjoy them, what could be better?

Let your children see the advantages of making your life easier. A Texas mother told her daughter she'd love to do more activities with her but had too much to do around the house. The daughter *volunteered* to help, and now the two have more time to go to movies and roller-skate.

The experience of a Pennsylvania working mom might be instructive. She had recently taken a job outside the home and was going crazy trying to fulfill all her responsibilities. So she communicated. Told her family she needed help.

All the family members wrote down on a sheet of paper things they'd be willing to do. Then her twelve-year-old daughter was told to "make like a computer" and give everybody a fair percentage of the work.

Every Sunday, each family member does seven things. The mother indicates it has fostered a *great* feeling of camaraderie. One Sunday, as she finished in the kitchen, Mom saw her daughter spontaneously helping her brother with his homework. "They worked together for *thirty minutes.*"

The mom writes, "This system may not be perfect, but it's close."

It may well be that such domestic tranquility is destined to elude us. But until we give it a try, we will never truly know for sure.

### POINTS TO REMEMBER

- When in doubt, delegate.

- Giving them chores is one of the best ways to teach children responsibility.

- Moms are not meant to be maids.

- Children should be in charge of their pets.

- Teenagers who are never required to vacuum are living in one.

- Occasionally, remind children tactfully that the oven is the only self-cleaning appliance.

# Weighing Every Word Makes
# Parents Speechless

REMEMBER WHEN PARENTS COULD "SAY it like it is"?

Now we practically have to *ooze* sensitivity. If a child swears at us, we have to praise him for "communicating." If he tells us to go to hell, we are to thank him for the travel opportunity.

Words do hurt, and we should try to speak respectfully to our kids at all times. If we call them "stupid," we are only demonstrating its genetic roots. But we can't *always* be 100 percent super-tactful and sensitive. We're human; we'll make mistakes occasionally.

Take a simple matter. Your daughter comes home from kindergarten with a drawing. Modern parents are instructed to praise the artwork and say, "Tell me about it." Good advice. But if we dare ask, "What is it?" we supposedly have harmed our daughter for *life*, despite our many daily sacrifices.

The simple act of answering questions has been raised to an art form. Only out-of-date parents actually *answer* questions from their children. We are to ask a question in return, to elicit our children's feelings, to encourage them to think for themselves. Let's do this *some* of the time. But if my parents had *always* answered my question with a question, nothing would more quickly have encouraged me to *stop asking questions*.

We can't talk directly! If we want our daughter to stay off the flowers, we can't say, "Please stay off the flowers!" We are to say, "I can't enjoy the flowers if they are trampled." Don't gently tell your child it is time for clean-up; inquire, "Can you show me where this truck goes?" It is forbidden to say, "If I catch you writing on the walls one more time, there is going to be a punishment." Instead, matter-of-factly say, "Walls aren't for writing. Paper is."

We're *never* to lie to our child. Okay, imagine if we adopt this literally:

HOW TO BE A HAPPY PARENT

Our child dresses in the morning, comes down to the breakfast table, and asks, "What do you think of my outfit?"

"I hate it," you respond. "I'll call Dr. Ramaker and make an appointment to check you for color blindness."

Over cereal your son practices his speech for first-period speech class.

"How'd it go?" he inquires.

"Well, there wasn't much content, your swaying made me dizzy, and I could barely hear you over the Rice Krispies. Other than that, it was one heck of a presentation."

Certain traditional phrases have become no-nos! It's wrong to say, "I'm proud of you." We're to say, "You must be proud of yourself." Never say, "I know how you feel." It's presumptuous. Watch out for "Why do you feel this way?" It puts our child on the spot. Perhaps he doesn't know why.

I conducted an experiment with my son Mike in the fine art of speaking sensitively. When Mike got home from school and announced he had received an A on a test, I was especially effusive. "Mike, you must feel very proud of yourself. Not every child can get an A. Your mother and I are very happy." He gave me a funny look.

Later that day, Mike struggled on the golf course. "Golf can be a very frustrating game," I said, giving his feeling a name. "Some people might be tempted to give up. Mom and I appreciate your persistence and love you very much." Again, a glance.

The next day Mike was walking to a lawn-mowing job and was pushing the mower in the street but on the side that allowed him to observe oncoming traffic. "It makes me very happy that you followed my instructions on how to transport your mower," I said. "Not all children are such good listeners." A look that could only kill.

Finally, that night we were going to a baseball game, and in the parking lot Mike used an especially sophisticated word. "What a colorful word," I complimented. "Not all children have such a wonderful vocabulary. Your mother and I are happy indeed to know such a wonderful speaker."

Mike had had enough. He began to hit me playfully. "Stop it," he said. "Whatever it is, stop it. Talk normal!"

Mike, I quite agree.

*Everyone* is in favor of children having high self-esteem. Unfortunately, there are no magic formulas to provide it.

### HOW TO BE A HAPPY PARENT

We certainly try hard enough. We hire a toy consultant to advise us on self-esteem-producing toys. We fax the four-year-old's drawing to Daddy in Paris. We allow our son to choose that horrible purple for his room. One book not only advises parents to know the names of their children's friends (certainly a good idea) but suggests that caring parents should be familiar with the names of their children's friends' *pets.*

We personalize *everything*—the book bag, the mug, the light switch, the lunch bag, the storybook, the lullaby, the ruler, the pencil, the clothes hanger, the T-shirt, the book cover, the bike license plate. Yet still the kid often doesn't know who he is.

We attend all our kids' athletic contests as well as "Meet the Teams" and end-of-season sports banquets. We yell, "Good try," every time our daughter's foot comes within eight feet of the soccer ball, and prepare a personalized newspaper headline that reads "ANDREW GETS A NO-HITTER!" when our son, the batter, goes 0 for the summer at Little League.

We let our child take part in many activities that *promise* to improve self-esteem. The fat camp. The tutoring service. The part-time job. The gymnastics and karate classes. The charm school. The sports camp.

Isn't it time to admit that producing self-esteem is a darn tricky concept? Take two brothers, twins if you will. Raised *identically.* Same hugs and kisses from their parents. Similar loving messages from teachers, clergymen, and coaches. Yet one can have high self-esteem, the other, not.

Look at all the hours our kids spent listening to Mister Rogers. Here was a wonderful, sensitive male who *daily* told our kids he loved them "just the way they are" and that it was a "good feeling" to know they're alive. If that didn't provide our kids with a lifetime of self-esteem nourishment, what can?

Many mental-health professionals feel self-esteem is in fact innate. Some people have it, others don't. The child with "everything" commits suicide; the youngster raised in an abusive, unloving home somehow thrives. The A student feels unworthy; a D student is confident and sure.

Some children seem oblivious of even major slights, while others are impacted by everything. A frustrated mom said to her six-year-old daughter, "You must have a small brain." Responded the daughter, without skipping a beat, "Of course I do, Mommy. I'm a small person."

Self-esteem used to be viewed as a core concept. It didn't fluctuate twice a week. If you had loving parents, all would probably be fine. Not so today. Self-esteem is viewed as *fragile*. Every disappointment or minor embarrassment can become a threat to it—if the child is eliminated first at dodge ball; has a lunch box unadorned by the hottest license; wears last year's jeans; owns a water gun with a shorter range than his neighbor's.

When we allow children to think that their core self-esteem fluctuates with such relative trivialities, aren't we helping to undermine it? Our kids don't live in a perfect world, and bad things will happen. Someone will have more action figures or a doll with a larger vocabulary. Teasing will occur; complexions won't always be clear.

I was at a baseball game recently where many middle-schoolers were in attendance. Whenever an imperfect female walked past, many boys would *moo* loudly. What dumb, hurtful, and obscene behavior. But it happens. Our children will be exposed to it. The key is to prepare them for it and educate them to rise above the momentary hurt.

Kids need occasional honest feedback. Used to be, when a child misspelled a word, we could just say, "That's incorrect." Now we must sugarcoat. "Well, that's one interpretation!" "Jason, you certainly are creative with your English." "Good try, but perhaps your teacher might be happier if the *i* was before the *e*."

Children do have different abilities, and we shouldn't be scared to acknowledge it. One child was speaking with a psychologist and was asked what sports he liked. "Baseball, but I'm not good at it," he replied. This supposedly demonstrated poor self-esteem. Maybe the kid *just can't catch,* and he should be complimented for his honesty. As long as he continues to play this sport that he enjoys, what's the problem?

The best way for children to develop self-esteem is for parents to *model* it. If the line is twelve deep for dessert at McDonald's, let the teenager stand in it. Parents can occasionally select the radio station in the car. If we find the time to deliver a forgotten lunch to school, let's also block out time for a lunch date with a friend. If mom hasn't bought a new dress in a decade, why must her daughter wear overpriced jeans?

One mother drove her child many miles *every*

*day* so that she could participate in ballet class. Mom was really looking forward to her daughter getting her driver's license. The day after she received it, the daughter quit the lessons. Why? She didn't want to do "all that driving."

I recently heard of an unbelievable case. A mom going through a divorce moved into a two-bedroom apartment with her two teenage daughters. Guess the sleeping arrangements. The oldest daughter has bedroom number one; the other child has bedroom number two. You can find Mom on the couch!

Tell the kids if they hurt your feelings. You prepare a nice meal and your son calls it "dog food." Or your daughter forgets your birthday. We want our kids to let us know when we hurt *their* feelings. Shouldn't it work both ways?

Look at what happens if a child swears at the referee during a soccer match. He'll miss his next game, and all of us applaud this sanction. So why does the child get off scot-free if he swears at us? Aren't we, the parents, entitled to as much respect as the ref?

It is time to level with the kids. Let them know that life will not always be fair. That words can hurt but needn't destroy. That children survive being cut from a team. That there will be other dances in their lives. That clothes don't make the man. That bosses aren't always reasonable.

And that even the best parents occasionally say dumb things.

## Points to Remember

- If self-esteem were easy to impart, everyone would have it.

- The more we shelter children from every disappointment, the more devastating future disappointments will be.

- It's hard to build bridges with a child hurling Legos.

- A parent who occasionally doesn't say something stupid to his child probably needs to converse more.

- Ignoring a child's disrespect is the surest guarantee that it will continue.

- Parents who expect perfection from themselves are setting themselves up for failure.

- Children are not the only important members of our households.

# Clothing a Child Shouldn't
# Give Parents the Shorts

HERE ARE CERTAIN CLASSIC WAYS TO TELL if fashion is playing too major a role in your child's life. Be concerned if your six-year-old daughter develops Imelda as a nickname. Likewise if the head of the regional shopping mall calls to ask your teenager if he will be in town the following weekend so "Fall Bonanza Week" can be scheduled.

Recently, I was interviewed by a journalist on the Gulf Coast of Texas. She had been anticipating a visit from her grandchildren, hoping to show off the beach and do some fishing. Know what the kids wanted to do? Visit the mall. The journalist remarked, "What is natural beauty without a food court?"

A Maryland teenager kept saying, "My wardrobe is so tiny, I can visualize *every* item." The next day her mom and dad started a clothing allowance for her.

Increasingly, our kids are walking billboards. They advertise all the "name" stuff. Shoes are Air Jordans. Jeans are Levi's. Fashion is everything. At a local grade school, a child who routinely stayed in at recess received a call from the president of Nike. He was told to get out, mingle with kids on the playground, or return his T-shirt!

Appearance is often more important today than performance. From talking to players after a baseball game, you would expect the box scores to appear in *Women's Wear Daily*, not *The Sporting News*:

"How'd the other team hit, son?" you inquire.

"It was a thrill just to watch them, Dad," comes the reply. "They had bats in six different colors and carry cases that *match*."

"Did they get their hands through the ball?"

"How couldn't they? They had jet-black batting gloves, *leather*-lined. A few kids even had a glove on *each* hand. Talk about intimidation!"

"How was their running game?"

"Out of sight. They had the special Nikes, with the all-purpose cleats. Bright red. Spanking-new. I hated to see them get dirty when they slid."

"How was their fielding?"

"You should have seen their gloves. Half the kids had Pump gloves. Out-of-sight. And great wraparound shades. Designer."

The fads our children chase are amazing. Take "button-fly" jeans. They were all a mistake. A worker in Taiwan forgot to order enough zippers and saw a crate of buttons left over from World War II. The rest is marketing history.

Stylish clothing creates special financial risks, also. A son bought an expensive baseball cap for $19.95. About a week later, the father remarked that he hadn't seen his son wear the cap for some time:

"Did you lose it?" his father inquired.

"Nope," replied his son.

"Is it defective?"

"No, it's fine," the son responded.

"Well, what's the problem?"

"It's out-of-date," the son sheepishly responded.

"Out-of-date?" Dad asked.

"Yup, out-of-date. Just my luck. The day after I bought it, the team changed its logo."

Unfortunately, the Major League teams are expanding more rapidly than our incomes. Florida gets a team? Buy a Marlins jacket. Colorado, too? Get a Rockies cap. The NBA expands? Get a Shaq attack.

You know, the pro teams are going about this in the wrong way. Whenever they want to raise money, they sell an individual franchise for many millions of dollars. But I'll bet that millions and millions of tapped-out parents would pay a few bucks apiece for the leagues *not* to expand.

What a shame to spend so much on clothing, since our kids grow so fast. One salesclerk asked the male teenager his size. "Today?" he responded. Often the clothing is too small by the time we receive the Visa bill.

Now that there is a preferred athletic shoe for every athletic activity, we're really in trouble. Shoes for wrestling on Tuesdays; volleyball on Thursdays; soccer on wet fields running north-south. Nothing more satisfying to a parent than seeing six pairs of athletic shoes outgrown simultaneously.

Children often are mystified by the word *sale*.

A shocking percentage truly believe it is a synonym for *free*, and have the mistaken notion that when you buy on sale, you are actually *saving* money. Wrong. You are *spending* money. And the supposed "savings" rarely materialize. "Mom, I can buy a pair of matching shoes with the money I *saved* on the dress."

Other terms also confound our kids. They see a sign, TWO-FOR SALE, and assume it's a bargain. Did the sign say two for *what*? Maybe it's just a mental processing thing, but I swear when kids see a sign, NO PAYMENTS TILL JULY, they understand that to mean, "No payments in my lifetime."

The whole jargon of shopping is a challenge. One dad, out shopping with his daughter, saw a sign, SWIMSUITS, HALF OFF. It was only when he saw the suit on his daughter that he learned that it referred to the amount of material, not the price.

A mom was walking with her daughter in the mall and spotted a rack of jeans, "$19.99 AND UP." Ah, the notorious UP. On the rack were one pair of $29.99 jeans, two at $39.99, and everything else far higher. The $19.99 pair? It had chocolate ice cream stains on the leg, a bent zipper, and pin holes left over from a KENNEDY FOR PRESIDENT button. It's time for merchants to come clean. Forget $19.99 AND UP. How about MAINLY $69.99 AND DOWN.

Prom expenses are increasingly out of control. Only the top-of-the-line tux will do; this from a son who has worn the same pair of Levi's for four years. One daughter, who couldn't tell Cornelius Vanderbilt from Gloria, couldn't live without the deluxe coordinated purse. Add the flowers, fancy halls, entertainment, and the obligatory limo, and it's amazing that any of these kids actually see college.

Parents nationwide are taking commonsense measures to bring fashion back under control. In the immortal words of a Connecticut mom, "A parent's job is to cover butt, not to decorate it." Many households set a reasonable limit on the price of athletic shoes. Anything beyond that, the child has to pay. I love a Missouri family's method of apportioning sneaker cost: the parents buy the right shoe, the child buys the left.

An Illinois woman staged an "Olympics" between an expensive pair of athletic shoes and a discount-store brand. She timed and measured her son in ten different events. Guess what? There was no difference in his performance, regardless of which shoe he was wearing. The child couldn't believe it. He repeated all the events, with his friend manning the stopwatch. Same results. It made a strong impression.

A New Jersey couple played "Sports Jeopardy" with their daughter. She wanted a Giants jacket, but it cost $120. Mom thought it was too expensive, but the daughter said, "You knew it would be expensive." The father told her that she could have the jacket if she could name five members of the Giants team. She could only name one.

Putting children in charge of maintaining some of their specialty clothing can work wonders. A Pennsylvania teenager insisted on clothes from a certain store. The problem was the label: HAND-WASH, DRIP-DRY, 100% COTTON. The mom allowed the child to buy them, but he had to wash and iron them. And in the Midwest, a child walked home in his socks rather than allow his expensive new tennis shoes to get muddied by the rain.

Explain to teenagers how one purchase affects another. One Christmas an Ohio teen spent all her money on expensive designer jeans. When she wanted other clothing later in the year, Mom reminded her that she had spent her money at Christmas. "Made her a much better shopper."

Kids will test us. A Kentucky child refused to wear *any* shoes that were within his mom's budget. So they left the shoe store with nothing, even though the child's everyday shoes had holes. Three days later, the child said he was ready to return to the store and buy something more affordable.

An Oregon mom bought her child a Nintendo game and some gym shoes for his birthday. The son was disappointed; he had wanted Pumps. The son "claimed" the shoes didn't quite fit right, and when they returned to the store, he tried to get his mom to trade up. Mom refused, but offered to return the video game and use that money to get the Pumps. The child said, "No way."

Don't let your kids work you over by misrepresenting what their friends possess. A teenager told her mother that her friend Angela was getting three-hundred-dollar winter boots "at the first sign of appropriate weather." In fact, Angela's mother told her daughter that she could get the boots "when hell freezes over!"

Having our children use their own money for a portion of their fashion needs teaches good lessons. A New Jersey mom requires her child to use birthday money for her clothing. The youngster had forty dollars, and when the sales clerk gave her thirty-four cents change, she asked, "Is this all I get back?"

But beware! A mom and daughter were to split the cost of a twenty-dollar accessory item. Mom gave her daughter ten dollars. But the item was on sale and only cost seventeen. Mom asked for her change. Without skipping a beat, the daughter responded, "Sorry, Mom, there is none. I spent your ten dollars first!"

Many families are moving toward clothing allowances. Children are given a certain amount of money to spend (for example, three hundred dollars for back-to-school clothes), and anything beyond that comes out of their pocket. It forces *them* to shop sales. To prioritize. To say no to themselves. And often they are allowed to keep any money left over.

Some families go with an *annual* allowance. Children are given their money at the first of the year. Mom and Dad might still pay for warm coats and hats and gloves (to be sure, they are bought), but otherwise the teenager is on his own. Might the teenager be tempted to spend all the money at once? Perhaps. But what a great way to learn. Every parent I've met who has his children on a clothing allowance *swears* by it.

An Indiana teenager rushed out to spend a year's worth of money on designer jeans. Then overnight he grew four inches. He wasn't willing to use *his* money for additional purchases, so he wore his short pants to school all year. Subsequently, he held money back for emergencies.

Popularity and fashion are transient things. What matters is what is inside our children, not on them. That's the message we should be teaching.

A young girl learned this the hard way.

She had been *dying* for a pair of designer jeans. These were beyond her parents' price range. Finally, Mom saw a pair on closeout and indulged.

The daughter was in heaven. She looked forward to wearing the jeans to school and receiving the jealous glances of others. It was all she talked about, and she modeled her jeans endlessly in her bedroom mirror. Finally, the special day came and she walked excitedly to school. But she returned in tears.

"What's the matter?" her mom inquired.

Replied the daughter, "No one even noticed."

HOW TO BE A HAPPY PARENT

## POINTS TO REMEMBER

- Children will always start a major growth spurt the day they get a totally new wardrobe.

- Proms should cost less than weddings.

- Parents' closets should always have more full hangers than their child's.

- Almost all clothing hassles will cease the instant you give your child a clothing allowance.

- Children who do their own wash will buy fewer garments that require hand-washing.

- The more "sales" you avoid, the more money you'll have.

- Today's fad is tomorrow's rummage.

# Teaching Right from Wrong Is More Important Than Teaching Right from Left

VALUES, VALUES, VALUES. WE'RE ALL ABUZZ about them. How to instill them? Teach them? Live them?

Trouble is, people of goodwill disagree on values. For example, some parents allow swearing in their homes, while others forbid it entirely. Some discuss sex early with their children, while others avoid the subject.

And there are so few absolutes. "Always tell the truth," we tell our kids. Yet don't we panic when we find that envelope from the IRS in our mailbox? When Grandma asks, "How did you like the fruitcake?" do we *really* want our kids to tell it like it is?

## HOW TO BE A HAPPY PARENT

And we all disagree on so much. Some of us are liberals, some conservatives. Some Democrats, some Republicans. Yet there are certain absolutes that unite us all. We uniformly want our children to be generous, kind, self-disciplined, to work toward a goal and think of others.

Values *are* important, and teaching them has never been more important. In the Midwest, two teenage girls came upon a large shopping bag, filled with Christmas presents, mistakenly left behind by a forgetful shopper. Instantly, they faced a classic moral dilemma. Do they keep all the presents, even though they all might not be the right size? Or do they return the individual items to the stores so they can receive the cash? The thought of turning the bag in to the lost-and-found never even *occurred* to them. Is there anyone of goodwill who isn't appalled by this story?

Our first line of defense in raising children with values is modeling good behavior ourselves. This is critical. How will our kids learn tolerance for others if our hearts are filled with hate? Learn compassion if we are indifferent? Perceive academics as important if soccer practice is a higher priority than homework?

We must model honesty for our children. Once

I took Mike to a rural park, to walk a scenic trail in search of pretty leaves for Mommy. As I drove into the unstaffed entrance, I came upon a sign that read, ADMISSION, $1. Even though there were many cars in the lot, there wasn't *one* envelope in the bin. What to do? So I discussed it with Mike. "Mike, the cars ahead didn't do the right thing. What should we do?" We quickly came to the correct decision; one hundred pennies never taught such a good lesson.

Several times I had to pay out on rash wagers. Once, at a Milwaukee Brewers baseball game, I said to Bob, "If you beat me to the top of the ramp [I was way ahead of him], I'll take you to every away game next year." Well, senile Dad forgot about the bet, and the little creep slipped past me. I was at his mercy. I explained that I couldn't afford to spend all next summer traveling. And I intimated that the state superintendent of public instruction would personally be monitoring his school attendance. So we settled for a three-day trip to Minneapolis to watch the Brewers.

The same disaster with Mike. We were going bowling, and this cocky six-year-old was "guaranteeing" me he'd get three strikes in a row. I said, "Mike, this is ridiculous. I'll pay you five dollars for two strikes in a row and *double* it every successive strike." How was I to know he'd throw a *five*-bagger?

Credibility is everything. Kids are like elephants; they never forget. A minister promised his son a new lawnmower, but for four or five years he never delivered. The son never brought up the subject. One day the minister was preaching the importance of keeping your word to a packed congregation. Suddenly, his son stood up and shouted, "Don't listen to him. He still owes me a lawnmower."

We *can* turn things around, both within our homes and in society in general. But we must work at it. Our kids will develop a work ethic only if we require them to pay a portion of the cost of some of the things they want. They'll learn to defer gratification the moment we stop routinely pulling out our wallets. And they'll learn self-discipline only if we care enough to enforce reasonable limits.

Respect is mandatory. Demand it. For yourself as well as for other authority figures in your children's lives, like teachers and clergymen. Let's always consider the "remote" possibility that the teacher's version of the incident is factual! Too often we buy into the child's excuses. "Okay, you didn't *throw* mashed potatoes in the cafeteria. You had WD-40 on your hands from shop class and the potatoes *slid* out." Sounds plausible to me.

Don't ignore youthful indiscretions; provide a lesson. A young child came home from the grocery store with watermelon seeds. He claimed the grocer, a family friend, gave them to him. The next time Mom was in the store, she playfully criticized the grocer for creating extra gardening work by giving her son the seeds. The grocer didn't know what Mom was talking about. The child had stolen the seeds.

Mom subsequently gave the child extra chores around the house, to earn money to pay for the seeds. And she required her son to deliver the money in person, and to apologize. Both the child and the grocer were in tears, but Mom reports her child "hasn't stolen anything again."

Too often we fear that informing our child of inappropriate behavior will undermine his self-esteem. This doesn't have to be. It never stopped our parents from teaching right from wrong. Certainly, don't belabor the point or make your child feel worthless or bad. Point out that you, too, made inappropriate decisions when you were young and are grateful to *your* parents for teaching what was correct. And let's remember that a child's knowledge that he *has values* will ultimately *bolster* self-esteem.

Keeping older kids on track is equally mandatory, though it's increasingly a challenge. Be prepared to be portrayed as the most unreasonable parent in the whole community, as your child assures you that *"everybody"* is doing it. Have you noticed that it's always *everybody*? Never half the kids, never three-quarters. Always *everybody*. Don't our educators teach fractions anymore?

One mom was told by her fourteen-year-old daughter that everybody was going to Florida over spring break. Mom checked it out, and no other parent had yet given permission. "It's worth the connection," this mom writes. "Now we could say that *'all'* the parents are opposed."

We must be willing to risk temporary unpopularity. A group of kids celebrating a bar mitzvah in a fancy restaurant started a food fight. Mom asked the manager for several trash bags and required the children to clean up their mess. Her daughters were embarrassed, but how can a true adult ignore such outrageous behavior?

A mom was dropping her daughter off at a

"small" party, and her daughter swore that the boy's parents were going to be home. When Mom arrived at the house, hundreds of teens were milling about and no adult seemed present. A young man approached the car and assured Mom that his parents would be home "any minute." The mother instructed the young man to call the instant his parents returned and in the meantime drove her daughter home. The phone still hasn't rung.

A group of kids was going to a motel after the prom. When they got there, they discovered the mom of one of the boys waiting, as a "volunteer chaperon." She spent the night with the kids, and the next day the kids presented her with a trophy for her effort: "World's Best Baby-sitter."

Four suitemates in college wanted their parents to pop for a four-hundred-dollar microwave. One set of parents objected, thinking it was unneeded. They prevailed upon their daughter for the phone numbers of the other parents. Guess what? They were all appalled by the price and were simply going along because they didn't want to appear not to be paying their fair share.

Many families have come up with special strategies to keep their kids on track, to help them avoid bad situations. In one household, a daughter asking permission in front of friends uses special words to indicate the answer she would like to receive. If she asks Dad, "*May* I go to the mall?" she wants a yes answer. But if she asks, "*Can* I go to the mall," she is looking for a no. And many families inform their children to claim they are grounded if they are invited to a party at which they think trouble might occur.

So often we doubt ourselves when it comes to values and fear that "only *we* feel this way." But almost always, the other parents feel just as we do. They are just scared to speak out. They don't want truly young children watching R-rated videos, either. They don't want to see risqué T-shirts on fourteen-year-olds, more stretch limos at the middle-school graduation, or beer logos on clothing worn by high-schoolers.

Let's remember to reinforce the efforts of those parents trying to instill values and responsibility in their children. A second grader deliberately broke a window at school while playing kick ball. He told his parents but said that they "shouldn't worry. Insurance will pay for it." The parents were appalled by the attitude. They made an appointment with the school principal and told him they wanted their child to pay for the window. Know what the principal said? "Don't worry. Insurance will pay for it."

Same for a friend of mine. His son lost half of his basketball uniform. Dad made an appointment with the coach and wanted his son to pay five dollars for the missing top. But when he was offered the money, the coach said, "Don't worry. These were old uniforms, anyway. Forget it."

So many kids are growing up in homes lacking caring parents that it is our *responsibility* to provide guidance. If you see unsupervised young children misbehaving, tell them to knock it off. If your son's friend is misbehaving in your house, inform him of the rules. Send him home if he persists. It might be the only structure the child knows, perhaps his only chance to learn what's appropriate. And it's great for your child to see that your values are so important to you that you require his friends to honor them.

We parents must have the courage to stand up for what is right. What do we want our kids to say to drugs? *No!* Well, they should hear us occasionally say no. Rather than feeling guilty when we stand up for principle, we should feel our proudest. And communicate to our children that we love them so much that we *must* make the right decision, not the easy or popular one. And that we expect them to show *similar independence* if some of their friends are making unwise choices.

When our kids are young, many of us rush out to buy a cute little baby book to record the meaningful events of our young child's life. The date he spoke his first word. The timing of the first tooth. Favorite kind of baby food. A first kiss. All important stuff. All good stuff.

But I've often thought there should be a second book, one with room to record the moral milestones of our child's life. There might be space to record the dates she first shared or showed compassion or befriended a new student or thought of sending Grandma a get-well card or told the truth despite its cost.

This second volume wouldn't take the place of the first book but would augment it. And, hopefully, supercede it as our child grows. For the first book records events that almost invariably happen. The second book reflects those events we would *like* to see happen. And, as such, constitutes the fairest possible gauge of the true success of our parenting.

FRED G. GOSMAN

## Points to Remember

- *Everybody* is never doing it.

- The fellow parent you are scared to call is as appalled by the clique's plans as you are.

- Most teachers don't have a picture of your child affixed to the middle of their dartboard.

- The other parent is as happy to hear from you as you would be to hear from him.

- Our kids will not be leaders if we are only followers.

# Watching Twelve Soccer Games a Week Is an Unreasonable Goal

**S**PORTS ARE *EVERYWHERE.*

Used to be, a father wished his child would become a doctor. Now, being a starting pitcher or a middle linebacker will be more than sufficient.

Even the terminology is invading our home. One mother asked her son why he was always irritating his sister, and he responded, "I'm the designated hitter." Another child, talking to the authorities, argued that he really hadn't run away from home. He had just "declared free agency."

The finest detail must be in place for athletic success. Once one of my kids was involved in a divisional play-off in our local Little League. One of the rival coaches happened to be warming up a relief pitcher, and the child threw a ball that barely missed me. I asked the coach to please move farther away. He said he could not, that he wanted the relief pitcher to be throwing in the *exact same direction* as he would be throwing in the game. Even Major League bullpens don't offer this luxury!

I was shocked during recent coverage of the Little League World Series. A radar gun measured the speed of every pitch. The coaches were miked up, so their conversations with their players were broadcast to millions. How would you have liked to be the starting pitcher getting shelled?

Did you see that article about the football coach at LSU? His squad was underperforming, and the coach moved into the athletic dorm "to get closer" to his players. Can you see a physics or history professor doing this?

And the price of all the sports equipment we buy! Go looking for a baseball bat with your child, and you're in trouble. He is convinced that he knows the *exact* bat he needs, with the latest features tailored to his game (including the politically correct player autograph). And he uses it proudly, until his first slump.

Coaches are, of course, wonderful people

who give selflessly of their time. But they're not always on top of *everything*. A second-stringer on an Oklahoma high school freshman football team was told by his coach to "go in for Douglas." Responded the startled child, "Coach, I am Douglas."

And all the clichés. Let's say the pitcher is walking lots of batters. To put it euphemistically, "he's having trouble finding the plate." To say it like it is, his pitches are landing in the next county. What sage advice do our coaches offer? "Throw strikes! Concentrate! Aim the ball at the target." Heck, I could have thought of that.

Sometimes we put up with things in sports that we wouldn't tolerate elsewhere. Once one of my kids was on his Little League All-Star team. Practices were on weekends and would start at three. No one was ever told when they would end. Parents began arriving at about five and would sheepishly wait till as late as six-thirty for their kids to be dismissed. Aren't families entitled to make weekend plans? If our son was taking violin or karate lessons, wouldn't we expect to know when the session would be over?

Today's kids evaluate coaches in ways that would make old-timers wary. Listening to future

Little Leaguers discuss their dream skipper is truly an education:

"I hope I get coach Smith. His van has Nintendo."

"True," pipes in another. "But don't forget most of our games will be at home. Coach Jones buys Big League chew for his players, in the flavor of their choice."

"Wow, I didn't know that," chimes in a third. "But I still might want Mr. Tucker. I hear his end-of-the-season barbecue is top-notch. His wife makes a baked-bean dish to die for."

The second child adds, "That's true, but I hear that coach Nelson has the biggest limit at Dairy Queen. On a hot day that is really nice."

"Big deal," the first child interjects. "Coach Reverand gives you cash for treats and allows you to keep the change."

"I forgot about that," responds the second. "I guess I'll go with him. That sounds like *my* kind of revenue sharing."

With all the commercialism, it's getting tougher and tougher to keep our kids innocent. In one of my son's Little League teams, an enterprising catcher sold advertising space on his jersey to a local dry cleaner! A manufacturer of anti-lice cream donated the batting helmets. And when one of the less skilled players somehow connected for a massive home run, his father initiated discussions with the Gerber people so that his son's likeness might adorn the label of "Baby Beets."

We go to many of the games, and often *our* personalities change the minute we hit the stands. Once at a basketball game I saw a Quaker yell, "Good foul," after his son sent an opponent to the hospital rather than allow him an uncontested lay-up. One sports-minded mom completely lost it. Her child loved to steal bases at baseball and was usually a walking grass stain after the game. One day the child tried to steal home. "Get down! Get down," the coach yelled, urging him to slide. Mom rose quickly from the stands, her face gripped with tension, and was last seen screaming, "Stand up! Stand up!"

Don't expect too much as a spectator. At baseball games, the ball is always hit to the position our child played *last* inning. At the end of the game our loved one will always be on-deck. And our child will always be playing the position where the sun is directly in his eyes.

Have you ever suffered through a season from hell? I did with my boys and their soccer team.

FRED G. GOSMAN

All *year* the ball was on *our* side of the field. The only time it wasn't, a sun-struck opponent mistakenly headed it in the wrong direction. Our team goalie entered therapy. The local grocer wouldn't sell us oranges. The select teams played videos of our games at their birthday parties.

Sometimes we wind up *hating* one of the kids. You know, the one who is a *disaster*. It's not that he makes "normal" errors. Half the team does that. He does *stupid* things. For example at baseball, he'll bang into the third baseman trying to catch a pop-up even though he's the right-fielder.

And worse yet, the kid is always *healthy*. Always there. The entire team might be down with intestinal flu, but this kid shows up with regularity. Talking to his parents is a downright effort. You say, "Skip is such a nice boy," but what you really would like to say is, "Why didn't you sign this loser up for soccer?"

All kinds of desperate thoughts cross your mind as the season unravels. You leave an anonymous message at his house that the game is cancelled. You request Community Services to mail him information on alternative programming. You take up a collection to send him to summer camp.

I love going to the games, but I'm still nostalgic

HOW TO BE A HAPPY PARENT

for the way it used to be. I was playing catch with Bob a while ago and reflected on the vast changes that have occurred.

"When I grew up, we played with neighborhood kids," I said.

"Who drove you to the field?" Bob asked.

"We didn't have a field. We played in the street, in front of our house."

"Well, who signed you up?"

"No sign-ups, Bob. Whoever wanted to play, played."

"Who hired the umps?" Bob inquired.

"There weren't any," I said. "We made our own calls."

"Come on, Dad," Bob responded. "How dumb do you think I am. Who made the calls?"

"Seriously, we did."

"And I suppose you're going to tell me you bought the uniforms, too!"

"We didn't have uniforms."

"What do you take me for? Why would you play if there weren't uniforms?"

"For the fun. Really, Bob. No uniforms. We dressed like we dressed. We could tell who was on our team."

"Well, who called practices?"

"Bob, we didn't have practices. We just loved to play."

"Who made you run laps?"

"There weren't any laps, though dashing to get the ball out of Mrs. Johnson's flower garden did improve our foot speed."

"Did you ever win a championship?"

"Bob, there were no championships. Just individual games."

"How many games in a season?"

"Bob, we didn't have a set number. If it was nice out, we played."

"How come Grandma never told me about these games?" he asked, sensing he had discovered my ruse.

"She never watched," I said.

"Come on, Dad," Bob exploded. "You're telling me that you played right in front of the house and Grandma never watched! She drives eight miles to see *me* play. Why are my games so much more important than yours?"

"Good question, son," I responded as I tried to surprise him by throwing a curve.

Isn't it time we leveled with our kids? Told them that the odds of a pro career are infinitesimally small. A Louis Harris poll in 1990 indicated that fully 32 percent of all male high school football and basketball players thought they could play professionally. Incredible.

Where are the brothers, and sons, of famous athletes? The relatives of Lou Gehrig, Stan Musial, Willie Mays, Harmon Killebrew, Mickey Mantle? They would have lots of advantages. Great genes. World-class instruction. Guaranteed tryouts with pro teams. If they can't make it, with *all that* going for them, what chance have most of our kids?

Let's start to get our sports back in balance. I love a story from the 1942 Rose Bowl. Due to wartime restrictions, the game couldn't be played on the West Coast. The players from Oregon State finally agreed to play at Duke, but only after receiving promises that they would be home in time for Christmas.

Some girls in West Virginia recently provided me with hope. They were on a high school softball team and, surprisingly, won some preliminary games in the state tournament. As a result of their success, they were scheduled to play in a regional final, but it conflicted with the senior prom. So the girls had to choose and, to their credit, chose the prom. Ladies, I salute you. If only more men had such perspective!

Often children participate in many sports activities solely because we make it so easy for them. An Idaho "sports chauffeur" was tired of spending more time in her car than at home. Just as an experiment, she required her children to pay half the cost of their sports activities. Guess what? The children cut down by 50 percent; they only participated in those activities they actually cared about. And filled their days by getting up games in their neighborhood.

I remember how often cars would interrupt our games when I was a child. Sure, we were upset at the drivers, but we always let them pass without incident.

I do a lot of driving. I never interrupt any game in progress. The kids aren't outside. They're inside, playing *at* sports. Watching ESPN. Slam-dunking on their Nintendo. Computing the current value of their baseball card collection. Waiting for their coaches to call a practice. And it makes me very sad.

Sure, we want our kids to "stay off the streets." But I'm not quite sure this is what we had in mind.

HOW TO BE A HAPPY PARENT

## POINTS TO REMEMBER

- Your child will always wind up using the base-ball bat of a teammate.

- Anyone sitting in the parents' section at a Little League game who evaluates the talent out loud will wind up friendless.

- Your child will always score the most goals the week you miss the game.

- The other mom's oranges are always juicier.

- If candy bar fund-raisers for athletic teams were outlawed, American obesity would decline by 93 percent.

# You Don't Need a Ph.D. to Outsmart a Child

FOR MOST OF US, IT'S NOT THE *BIG* THINGS THAT cause frustration. It's the little things.

The five hundred *why*'s an hour. Tantrums. Arguments over who goes first. Misbehavior in the car. Our five-year-old's conviction that it's *her* shopping trip and that *we* are the ones along for the outing.

Certainly, there are strong-willed children who can make any technique problematic. But for most of us, our neighbors might just have the solution.

## TANTRUMS

Tantrums are the Lord's way of protecting us from overpopulation. The trick, hard though it is, is to ignore them. When our children see they aren't getting our attention, they will calm themselves down. A Connecticut dad writes, "I let my child scream it out. The more I ignore it, the shorter it is."

And kids don't like going to all the effort without getting a favorable result. A child was hysterical in the grocery store because his mother wouldn't buy watermelon. After three minutes of being ignored by his mom, the child asked, "Am I going to get that watermelon? I'm getting tired of crying."

A New Mexico mom times tantrums on her watch. Roots her child on, to set a personal best. A Washington mom turns the table and stages her own tantrum, complaining bitterly about having to make lunch. Her daughter begins to laugh and soon is under control. A Missouri family made a sign, TANTRUM IN PROGRESS, and displays it at the toy store if necessary; because the parents feel less embarrassed, the child stops his tantrum sooner.

Of course we can't *always* ignore the tantrums: the minister might not approve. But the less fearful we are of them, the fewer there will be.

And occasionally sheer chutzpah might be required. A five-year-old was throwing a terrible tantrum in the grocery store. She lay down in the middle of the aisle and was yelling, kicking, and screaming. Know what Mom did? She lay down in the aisle right next to her daughter. And started yelling, kicking, and screaming. Within *ten seconds* her daughter stood up and said, "Mom, this is embarrassing. Let's go!"

## Time-outs

Short time-outs, with strict rules, are probably preferable to longer ones. In some homes, whenever the child talks during one or inquires, "How much time is left?" an extra minute is added to the time-out. Some children are required to stand during brief time-outs. In a Long Island family, the kids all have their own little time-out benches. They plan on saving them for *their* children.

Have a special time-out area, in a boring place. *Not* the bedroom though; there are too many sources of fun there. One Idaho mother uses the dining room. Her child complained, "But, Mom. There's nothing to do there." Replied the mom, "That's the idea."

Getting the child *into* time-out is not always

child's play. Go with the program of a Michigan couple. They start counting to five the second the time-out is announced. For every second longer it takes the child to get to the time-out area, an extra minute is added. And have time-outs apply to all. A Wisconsin father was assessed a five-minute time-out for burping at the dinner table!

One California family has a cute tradition, which seems to work for no good reason. The child serves his time on the stairs leading to the second floor. The worse his behavior, the higher the stair he has to sit on. The family reports that the child's behavior improved so he could avoid the higher stairs.

## WHINING

I have an idea for law-enforcement personnel. You know when they pipe in loud rock music in order to disorient the bad guys during a hostage crisis? They could do better. I say, *Pipe in whining*.

An Oregon family pretends their ears only hear pleasant voices and *ignores* whining totally. They claim it works perfectly, though it's hard to do. A New Mexico mom responds to whining by putting on earmuffs. A Maine dad whines right back, and claims success. A New Jersey father recorded the whining on a tape recorder and played it back for his son. A Wisconsin mom cured restaurant whining by claiming the family was seated in a NO WHINING section.

For a *very* whiny son, a Kentucky family set aside a "Freedom to Whine" day. The son could *only* whine and was playfully chastised when he spoke pleasantly. Sounds offbeat, but the parents say that nothing was as effective at helping their child differentiate pleasant from unpleasant communication.

Consequences can affect speech patterns. A Connecticut family chops ten minutes off bedtime for every whine. "On *The Simpsons* night we get very little of it." Check marks were the answer in a Florida home. Each whine gets a check mark. When they total five, the daughter goes a day without TV. "It's been two weeks now, and my daughter still has only the four check marks she received the first day."

A Missouri family reports great success with a "whining towel." The child is allowed to whine but must get a special towel and place it around his neck when he does. He so hates going to get that towel that he generally settles down quickly.

HOW TO BE A HAPPY PARENT

## BEDTIME

Most of our young children seem to have developed an affinity for late-night TV. But bedtime doesn't always need to be a hassle.

A Texas family grew tired of the long litany of complaints their child reserved for bedtime. "My stomach hurts! I need a glass of water!" They set aside a period fifteen minutes *before* bedtime. The child could choose either to play during this period or to air all his complaints. Grumbling quickly disappeared.

One dad, tired of nightly battles, allows his child to stay up, but the youngster must help with chores; bedtime has been a lot smoother ever since. Try role-playing. Let the child be the mom or dad, and you be the kid. Have the youngster try to get you down for the night. Or simply allow the child to stay up. One Nebraska mom told her eight-year-old that he would have to stay up three more hours, until her bedtime. "After fifteen minutes, he was *begging* to be allowed to go to sleep."

Of course, some shenanigans are to be expected at bedtime. But if there is a real problem, tomorrow's bedtime is often the answer to tonight's. Let your child know that every minute past five that he delays will be deducted the following evening.

One Louisiana family staged a scene to drive this point home. Might seem cruel, but it *was* effective. Their child had stalled mercilessly the night before, for forty-five minutes. The parents said bedtime tomorrow would be earlier.

That next evening, Mom and Dad suggested a board game about an hour before the normal bedtime. After just fifteen minutes of play, Dad "suddenly" remembered the earlier bedtime. The child went to bed with tears in his eyes. But the family reports it was the last time bedtime was a serious problem.

## POOR TABLE BEHAVIOR

What a shame to spend valuable time preparing a meal and have it ruined by misbehavior. Of course, true tykes have trouble sitting, and problems should be expected. But we shouldn't allow older children to spoil our meal.

Kids often try to get their "yucks" at our expense. Of course they should be allowed to indicate if they don't like something, but they should do so respectfully. A Michigan family has their "yucker" prepare his own meal for two straight nights. An Idaho couple requires their son to do the dishes.

Isolating a misbehaving child frequently works well. A Florida family makes the misbehaving child eat alone, in a different room. A Colorado girl was dispatched to the basement. A Pennsylvania child had to return to the table when the others were through and eat his meal *cold*. Sounds harsh, but these measures only had to be imposed *once*.

A Rhode Island family rewards the best-behaved daughter with a queen's crown left over from Halloween. She gets to wear it all night and is in charge of choosing the evening snack. Very effective.

Some kids seem to confuse dinnertime with gym class. One Montana family gave each child five pennies at the beginning of the meal and took one away each time the child got up. After a week, the children were sitting through their meals.

Sometimes *try* a new approach; miracles happen. A Minnesota family had a very active child who would parade all over the house during dinner. They improvised. The child was allowed to get up *once* during the meal. After that, his chair was taken away and he had to *stand* for the remainder of the meal. To the parents' amazement, by the second evening, their child was sitting *through the meal.*

But you must hear about the ceramic pig. Works wonders for an Ohio family. If a child (or adult) misbehaves at the table, the ceramic pig is placed in front of him. If someone else subsequently misbehaves, the pig moves to that person. Whoever has it at the end of the meal does the dishes.

A New York woman adopted a simple but highly effective approach. Her three- and six-year-old were "destroying" mealtime. So she had the two children eat late, at eight o'clock at night, while she and her husband ate together at their normal hour. Mom made sure the table was set very attractively, and prepared especially tasty dishes. The children so resented "missing the party" (as well as their bedtime snack), that within two days their behavior was much improved.

## Too Much Television

We all want our kids watching less TV. Many families impose a designated quiet time during weekday nights, from seven to nine P.M. No TV, no phone calls. And it applies to the parents, too. This is special time for homework, paperwork, and reading.

A Michigan couple with a VCR forbids their children from watching TV during weekday evenings. But the children can tape *as much as they want* and catch up on the weekends. You can guess what happened. The first week, the kids spent Saturday and Sunday in front of the tube. But subsequently they were involved in weekend activities and never found time to watch their tapes. Within a month, they barely taped at all.

Having the children merely write down the names of the programs they watch cut viewing by 50 percent in a New Hampshire home. "Kids just hate to write," reports the dad. Some families give out a number of tickets, or poker chips, which entitle their kids to a specific amount of TV. Additional tickets can be earned, and existing tickets lost, depending upon behavior.

Many families link TV viewing to other, more desirable activities. In a Maryland home, an hour of homework earns an hour of TV (news and educational programs are free). Reading a book earns two hours. The mother reports that the children rarely miss a favorite program and "actually enjoy the balance in their lives."

An Illinois family gives rewards for reduced TV viewing. If the children average less than an hour a day, they are taken to the roller-skating rink on Saturday morning. One child can go, or both. "It depends on what they decide is most important."

## CAR BEHAVIOR

Poor behavior in the car is especially maddening. I'm embarrassed to admit that during a trip to visit Grandma, I twice threw my copy of *365 Ways to Amuse a Child* at my kids. And we were still in the garage!

Children always want to know: "How much longer is it?" One family gives the children a map and encourages them to trace the route—a good idea. Express time in young kids' terms. Don't say, "An hour and a half." Why not say, "Three *Barneys*."

Quiet games can help. Give each child a Life Savers candy and see who can keep it the longest. One family plays a game they call "Status." The last one to speak wins, gets a little prize.

HOW TO BE A HAPPY PARENT

In a Michigan family, misbehaving children have to sit on their hands. The dad writes, "It's hard to talk without your hands!" A California mom merely pulls over to the side of the road and begins to read when her kids misbehave (she always keeps reading material in the glove compartment).

I love what an Illinois family does. At the start of a vacation, the parents give each child a roll of quarters to be used for video games or whatever. But each time they misbehave, a quarter is taken away.

If you try to have your young children play games during the ride—for example, finding license plates from all fifty states—have them cooperate. Give a reward if they accomplish the goal *together*. It makes for a more pleasant trip.

A mom with children who *perpetually* misbehaved wins our prize for creativity. The family was planning on driving from Virginia to Florida to visit Grandma, and Mom warned the children that if they misbehaved in the car, the trip would be cancelled. The children loaded up the car with suitcases, and the family departed. *Seven blocks* away from their own garage, Mom *cancelled* the trip.

At first the children thought their mother was bluffing. But when she drove home and asked them to unload the suitcases, they knew they were in trouble. All week they *begged* for another chance. The kids even called Grandma to ask her to put in a good word. Mom eventually relented; they made the trip the following weekend and she had "nine hundred miles of heaven!"

What the children don't know is that the initial trip, the week previous, had been a total and complete *fraud*. Mom had filled the suitcases with books, had fully expected to turn around, and the family arrived at Grandma's on the exact date they were due.

## TAKING TURNS

Fighting over who sits in the front seat has probably caused more accidents than faulty brakes. Here is the answer: Alternate months or weeks or days. Kids know it's fair. And maybe proclaim the child "Kid of the Week," so he feels truly special. Many families assign special responsibilities, like helping to set the table, to the child who gets to sit in the front seat. Perhaps worth considering.

Have a child who *always* has to go first? A New York parent told her daughter that since she loved going first, she would be "first to bed." "Me first" stopped really fast.

## SIBLING RIVALRY

Few things drive parents as crazy as sibling rivalry. But kids will always be kids!

A Connecticut woman was playing bingo and an elderly gentleman asked her son what he would do if she won twenty dollars. The child responded, "Buy an orphanage and put my older sister in it."

A New York mom was preparing for a rummage sale, and her two kids started fighting. The younger one went up to Mom and suggested putting a price sticker on her brother and selling him for fifty-nine cents. A New Jersey seven-year-old was picking on her two-and-a-half-year-old brother. Finally, the little youngster burst out, "Stop it! You can't do this to me. I'm a baby."

Siblings will probably always squabble. But there are ways to contain it. You *can* get rid of the unflattering names they use to describe each other. Anytime you hear your child use one, assess a one-dollar fine, with the money going to the child who was called the name!

Some families require squabbling youngsters to sit on the "love seat" till they have resolved their difficulties. Some require the offending child to say three good things about his sibling. Others forbid the kids from having playmates over. In a California home, "if they're not bleeding," the parents don't want to hear about it. An Oklahoma couple dispatches the youngsters to a distant room so the disagreement isn't dignified with an audience.

A California mom invokes a "silence contract" whenever her children bicker. The first one to speak helps with dishes, laundry, or "the task du jour." And in Wisconsin, one family completely separates squabbling siblings for two *full* days, even during meals. Writes the mom, "Their behavior always improves once they realize they have more fun together than apart."

Some families require their siblings to kiss each other after they fight. Another actually ties them together and requires them to remain like that for fifteen minutes. Look out for forcing children to be affectionate to each other. If I were the kid, these approaches would breed only resentment.

One family confronting siblings who always tattled came up with an effective solution. Anyone who tattled had to follow his sibling around for four hours and report on *everything*. Problem solved.

I think there are two methods to cure sibling rivalry. One approach is to give the children a chore. Routinely. "If you have time to fight, you have time to help out." Kids can still argue among themselves, but when they know that if *you're* involved they'll be cleaning a bathroom or washing windows, complaints will be few and far between.

Or you might try this approach from the state of Texas, where two sisters made the Alamo look like a tea party. Whenever they would complain to their parents, the two girls were required to write a fifty-word description of the incident so that the parents could, ostensibly, determine who was the guilty party. The girls so *hated* preparing these summaries that they stopped most of their fighting.

Sometimes we tolerate sibling bickering because we don't want to punish the child who is good. Let's say you've promised going to McDonald's as a reward and only one of the kids misbehaves. What to do? I suggest you take both kids to McDonald's, but have the misbehaving child *watch* as you and your other child enjoy your Big Macs and fries. Make the misbehaving child a peanut butter and jelly sandwich at home and, hopefully, behavior will improve quickly.

## PUTTING THINGS AWAY

Isn't it incredible the public relations effort that encourages parents to buy toy chests? Think about it. Why else would we routinely buy a piece of furniture whose sole purpose is to allow us to complain that it is not used?

An Illinois woman invented a "Mommy Box." Any toy not put away by the end of the day goes there. In order to get it back, the child has to pay a fine of a quarter. If you don't like fines, perhaps adopt a rule that anything put into the "Mommy Box" stays there for two days. Or require an extra chore.

Have the children get involved in cleanup. One Connecticut mom requires her children to clean up the basement if it isn't left neat. "Now my nine- and eleven-year-old start yelling at their friends if they try to leave before the basement is cleaned up."

If older children are leaving things around the house, such as the omnipresent book bag, you might try the approach of a Virginia parent. After tripping over it sixteen times in a week and after issuing six warnings, Mom hid the bag. Took her daughter twenty-five minutes to find it. Now she places it on the bench, where it belongs.

## POOR BEHAVIOR AT THE GROCERY STORE, MALLS, OR RESTAURANTS

The solution is simply not to reward inappropriate behavior. Don't buy treats for misbehaving children. Follow through once, and they'll behave next time. Or let your child know ahead of time of a reasonable consequence if his behavior is not up to snuff.

Perhaps you can have a tradition where good behavior at the grocery store is rewarded with a Coke at McDonald's. At shopping malls, many families reward their child with a purchase at the dollar store. But always have the child go without if he elects to misbehave.

A Florida couple has an unusual cure for problems at the mall. They tell their kids that if they continue to misbehave, they have to hold hands. A tad embarrassing and maybe not a great idea, but they say it works wonders. Another couple responds to misbehavior by breaking into song.

A Colorado dad has great success just talking to the kids. He calmly bends down to their level and asks, "Do you see any *adults* acting this way?" Says it works marvels.

An Indiana couple swears by its cure for misbehavior in restaurants. They keep reading material in the car. If the child is misbehaving, he is warned and then taken to spend some time in the car with a parent. They don't even have to threaten their son anymore. The parents just ask each other, "Whose turn is it to do car time?" and the children behave. Or you can always say, "If your behavior doesn't improve, we'll leave," and follow through *once*. Yes, it will be inconvenient. But if it assures appropriate behavior in the future, what an investment!

## SCHOOL HASSLES

Just getting kids to school is often a major undertaking. Kids routinely fall victim to "school-bus fever" and develop mysterious illnesses the instant they wake up. It's tough for us to know if the child is really sick or just faking. Many families take the empirical approach. If there isn't a temperature, the child goes to school (though he is free to call later in the day if he is not feeling well).

A Missouri mom always makes sure the first day at home consists of nothing but bed rest. If staying home means unlimited TV, Nintendo, and video rentals, why wouldn't it be more attractive than Mrs. Smith's math tables?

Missing the school bus is the favorite activity of some of our young ones. An Ohio mom keeps track of the extra minutes required to drive her daughter to school, and that evening the girl owes Mom three times that number of minutes in chores. Several families required their child to *pay* for the taxi that took them to school when they missed the bus. Only happened *once*. Other children are told that a day missing the bus is a day without television and video games.

Successful completion of homework is difficult if your child doesn't know his assignment. Many parents physically inspect the assignment notebook each night. If it is forgotten at school, the child is required (where possible) to walk back to school and get it.

Failure to hand in homework should be treated seriously. Of course, check for vision and like problems. But if there are none, make a statement.

An Indiana mom told her son that every missed assignment meant he'd miss part of his basketball game. A Kentucky parent required her fifteen-year-old daughter to wait an extra week to get her learner's permit for every missed assignment. In New York, a third grader learned that a missed assignment meant a week without TV. In all three cases, turning in work became a habit.

Don't immediately help your child, but give him a few minutes to find the answers himself. We can only do so much. One mother quit doing the child's homework, and the child's grades suffered. Most of his friends made the honor roll, and he did not. "It was the best thing for him," writes the dad. "He took charge of his own affairs, and improved his grades dramatically."

People of goodwill disagree on whether to pay kids for grades. Some think the good grade is the ultimate reward. But some kids *are* motivated by rewards. A Montana woman told her daughter she could have her own phone line if her grades improved. The daughter produced her best grades ever. Likewise, an Ohio high-schooler really dedicated himself to his studies when he knew a B average was his admissions ticket to summer soccer camp.

I have a confession. My parents paid me for good grades. But then again, I have another confession. That never cost them much!

## DATES WHEN PRIVILEGES START

Very often children drive us crazy, wanting to get pierced ears while still in diapers and wanting to watch R-rated videos at their fifth-birthday party. The key is to be fair. Set reasonable dates at which designer jeans, makeup, dating, and other privileges will begin. But don't allow your child to persist in trying to get these prematurely. At some point, you have to stop the harassment. Let them know that every time the issue is brought up, the privilege will start two weeks later.

## MISCELLANEOUS

There are thousands of ingenious approaches out there to handle most of our problems. One mom, confronting "constant why's" came up with the "Five-Why Rule." If a child asked "why" twice, she had to ask why three more times. The child hated it. Asking why became history.

Have a child who consistently forgets lunch at home? A Virginia middle-school mom grew tired of her needless trips to school and developed a plan. The next time her daughter called, the mom took the lunch to school. But her hair was in *rollers*; she was still in her *bathrobe* and was wearing *house slippers*. She introduced herself to the principal, and together they walked to her daughter's homeroom. She rapped loudly on the door, walked up to her open-mouthed daughter, and said, *"Here is your lunch."*

Many of us are torn apart when our children say, "That's not fair." We immediately begin a lengthy review of our actions for the last decade, in a vain attempt to assure our child of our impartiality. A Florida mom tries this approach: When her child says, "That's not fair," she responds, "You're right," and changes the subject. She says it works every time.

A parent with a bossy child found an excellent solution. Near day's end he gets a half hour of "Boss Time" to make the rules. The child loves it.

And he behaves, because otherwise he doesn't receive it.

Often, children try to wear us down by asking repeatedly for something, wanting an instant answer, or trying to embarrass us by asking questions in front of their friends. In a Michigan family, children are only allowed to ask twice for something. If they ask a third time, the no applies to the next day also. An Alabama family informs the children that if the answer *must* be immediate regarding some future plans, it will always be no. And many families insist that if a question is asked in front of a friend ("Can Bill eat over?") the answer is likewise no.

One family denied soccer practice to their child, but thought the consequence had little impact. The child merely stayed at home and played Nintendo. So the next time they had their son sit on the sidelines and *watch* his teammates practice. Behavior improved rapidly.

An Illinois woman had two children who refused to send relatives thank-you notes for checks. This situation cleared up quickly when Mom ruled that the checks couldn't be cashed until the notes had been sent.

A single mom with two sons confronted a real

problem. The nine- and twelve-year-old always tried to make her feel guilty when she left on a date. "Please, Mommy, don't leave us." She got even. One day her oldest was picked up by a friend after school to go skate-boarding. Mom allowed her son to get about forty feet from the house and then dashed after him and threw her arms around him. "Please, Josh, don't leave me!" she exclaimed. Her son responded, "Mom, this is silly!" Replied the mom, "I agree."

Quick thinking will cure more than an occasional problem. A family went with the grandparents to a theme park. The daughter refused to hold hands or to be tied. The family was afraid of losing her. "So we tied her to Grandpa and told her to be sure that he didn't get lost." She took it very seriously.

One family that was tired of complaints about "iron-hand" discipline dispatched their children to a relative's home, where the rules were even stricter. Another regales the kids with "horror stories" of what happened when they misbehaved as kids. "After hearing our embellished stories, the kids are pretty comfortable with the way we handle things. Our five-year-old often comes back for more stories about how *awful* our lives used to be."

An Iowa family uses a "Fair-Exchange Jar," and I think it's a great idea. If the child does something good, it is noted on a slip of paper and put in a jar. Same thing if the child does something not so good. Then if he asks for a special treat, one of the slips is drawn. If it notes positive behavior, the child gets his wish. But if it is negative, the answer is no.

Let's remember that it is wonderful to catch our children being good. Many families use rewards in very effective ways. In a Colorado family Friday is "Movie Night," but the activity is cancelled if misbehavior was common during the prior week. In Illinois, positive behavior in one home results in a scoop of beans being placed in a large jar. When it is full, a treat is due.

A Pennsylvania couple had children who nagged and nagged about going to a video-game parlor. The parents presented them with a plastic bag of tokens at the beginning of the month. Every time they misbehaved, they had to give one back. The mother writes, "What a month!"

A New York family uses "Happy" and "Sad"

cups to help their children with behavior. They add Popsicle sticks to each cup depending on behavior. At the end of the day, if the "Happy" cup has more sticks than the "Sad" cup, the children earn a Popsicle. If at the end of the week they've earned Popsicles six out of seven days, the family gets a new box of Popsicles and starts over.

A New York mom gives her children a penny each time she catches one of them doing something terrific; when the kids together have amassed sixty cents, they all go out for pizza. She also does something especially clever. Uses a sixty-three-piece jigsaw puzzle. A piece is handed out for exemplary behavior. Treats are doled out when the puzzle is completed.

I love the way one family keeps track of behavior. Rather than negative, the categories are positive: "respectful," "responsible," and "fun to be with." It is probably a good reminder for us all.

Hopefully, we can cure many of the minor aggravations that confront us and sleep a little more soundly at night. But don't sleep too deeply. You never know what the children might be up to!

HOW TO BE A HAPPY PARENT

## POINTS TO REMEMBER

- The only sure cure for sibling rivalry is to have *one* child.

- Your youngster will *eventually* fall asleep.

- The greater the number of toy shelves, the higher the percentage of toys on the floor.

- The Lord invented the "terrible twos" so parents would be sure to appreciate three-year-olds.

- If you always take skips, don't expect your children to take turns.

- Never entrust the remote control to someone under ten.

- Praise your child often, and good behavior will likely become automatic.

# Teenagers Almost Always
# Improve with Age

HAVE YOU NOTICED THE IRONIES OF LIV-
ing with a teen?

Your daughter hasn't the patience for homework but stands in line hours for concert tickets.
Your son perennially starts his shower the *instant*
before you do. The sixteen-year-old tries to wear
his "Co-Ed Naked Sunbathing" T-shirt to church
yet complains about *your* clothing.

Keeping informed of academic progress is increasingly problematic during these years. One
child kept telling his parents that he was getting
100's on his tests, so the folks relaxed. Turned out
he received a D. The perplexed parents confronted their teen: "What happened? You said

you were getting hundreds." "I was," responded the child. "Two fifties, three forty-fives, and a six. That's hundreds in my book."

Almost makes you feel foolish buying that study desk. Remember when the fourteen-year-old begged and begged? Listed all the advantages? Thus far, the struggling scholar has used it twice, and he still does his homework on the kitchen table.

When it comes to homework, our kids have time management down to a science. Say they have an hour of homework. They spend twelve minutes complaining about it. Seven sharpening pencils. Four finding the assignment notebook. Three indicting the lighting. Nine selecting the accompanying snack. Two finding paper. Three hunting down the eraser. Eight criticizing you for not taking the subject when you were in school. When they find they don't have enough time to complete their work, they assure you it will be done in study hall. Right. And the check is in the mail!

If they receive an A on a test, they proudly take individual credit—"I *got* an A." But if the results are less impressive, they shift—"The teacher *gave* me an F." The best spin is always put on every

FRED G. GOSMAN

poor grade. "Hey, I was only eight points away from a C," your son brags. "Correct," you counter, "but you were also one point removed from an F."

Teens often *live* on the phone. You've even stopped answering it—it's never for you. You'd call the Parents' Anonymous helpline for advice, but your line's always occupied.

Money becomes a sore point during these years. Have you noticed how teenagers often forget their wallet when they are out with you and want to make a purchase? How come they remember it when they go out with their friends?

Every expenditure *you* pay for is preceded by the word *only*, as if it's a formal rule of grammar. "Hey, Mom, these tennis shoes are 'only' a hundred bucks." "Hey, Dad, this stereo is 'only' five hundred and ninety-five dollars." I love the approach of one Maine dad. Whenever his child uses the word *only*, she gets to pay for it.

Driving a group of teens is a *real* joy. Rule number one: Keep your mouth shut. No questions. No comments. No jokes. No singing. No humming. If you can avoid the sound of your breathing, so much the better. Run *all* the yellow lights, or

HOW TO BE A HAPPY PARENT

you'll be called a wimp for driving conservatively. If you have to tell one of the passengers his shirt is on fire, do it quickly, nonjudgmentally, and as concisely as possible.

Once they get their driver's license, teens have a love affair with cars. You know, *cars*, the things we used to have available to drive.

I love what one Michigan family does. They never ground the kid. They ground the *car*. Works "really well." I also love the practice of a California couple. They routinely buy their kids a car when they turn sixteen, but a *very* inexpensive one. If the child goes a year without causing an accident or receiving a ticket and keeps his grades up, he receives a nicer one.

Speeding tickets can be an expensive problem. One father tolerated no Saab stories, and required his son to pay them. Turned out, the child worked, had money, and this strategy didn't change his driving habits. Then Dad hit upon the solution. Whatever the ticket cost, the child couldn't use the car for that many days. "Got my son's attention real fast."

Curfews produce their own crises. Above all, be clear. An Indiana child was going out for the

FRED G. GOSMAN

evening at seven o'clock, and Mom said, "Return by one." How was the child to know she meant A.M.?

I love the trick of a Montana family. As their children grew older, the parents found it tougher and tougher to stay up to wait for them. So they put an alarm clock outside their bedroom door, set for the curfew hour, which their children were to turn off. If the alarm sounded, the next curfew was an hour earlier.

Older teens, and young people in their early twenties, truly keep all hours, and this can worry parents. One family confronted their son, who wouldn't communicate when he was going to be out all night. The parents hadn't a moral problem; they simply were tired of worrying. So they adopted this system. They began to charge him three hundred dollars a month rent. However, it was reduced by ten dollars every day they were informed of their son's plans.

High-tech gear is a rite of teenhood. Why do manufacturers even bother to make low-volume settings on the stereo or boom box? The kids never use them. Our "unmaterialistic" son spends half his life in the local electronics store. The CD tower is taller than he is.

HOW TO BE A HAPPY PARENT

Even though all their gear has to be interactive, many teens rarely open their mouths. The daughter who used to tell us everything now whispers on the phone. Teen boys can go months without speaking. I feel lucky if I'm able to start the day by hearing a grumpy, "Give me the sports."

I was over at a friend's house and learned that his daughter was taking U.S. history. I was a history major, so I foolishly asked what she was studying. Know what she answered? "Chapter Twenty-three!" End of discussion.

My son Bob set the language back a few years when we recently dined in a Thai restaurant and he interfaced with an American waiter:

"What would you like to drink?" the waiter asked.

"Mountain Dew," Bob replied, mumbling.

"Pardon me?" responded the waiter.

"Mountain Dew," Bob repeated.

"Please, one more time," the waiter pleaded.

"Mountain Dew," my son said, as slowly as possible.

The waiter gave up. "I'm sorry," he said. "I don't speak Thai."

Inevitably, we are the least reasonable parents in our child's clique. All their friends have later curfews, bigger allowances, greater freedom, fewer chores. All receive more respect, more gifts, and more praise. Everybody has a fuller closet, a nicer car, and less embarrassing parents.

Teen years are tough. We must get through these years without permanently damaging our relationship. Kids are, well, kids. We need to be sympathetic. Understanding. Reasonable.

Lay off the room. It's theirs. So what if it would offend a toxic-waste inspector? Many kids are slobs when young, neat when older. The more we complain, the more they'll scatter.

A father asked me what could be done with his daughter. She was an honors student, popular, and respectful to adults. But she kept a messy room. My advice? "Count your blessings."

Teens' hairstyles have caused parents more than one post-part-em depression. Again, lighten up. It's their hair. All your carping will only re-inforce the style. You might care to try a different tack. *Compliment* your teen on his or her look; say it's growing on you. Nothing will likely cause him to change it faster.

Young adults deserve privacy. Let them open their own report cards, choose their own gradu-ation picture, elect how their name is officially listed on the graduation program. Always knock on their door, and wait for acknowledgment, before entering. Let them open their own mail. Don't drive them crazy with questions. We want them to open up, but forcing them to speak only lengthens the silences.

Remember to praise, even if it is forced. Laud your daughter's efforts to improve her voice, even when her efforts result in a drinking-glass shortage around the house. Praise your son's new shirt, despite your sudden lament that you don't suffer color blindness.

Be realistic about grades. Don't expect A's from a child whose bowling average is higher than his combined SAT's. Reward effort, even if the grades don't follow.

A child had a horrible time with geometry. He couldn't visualize the stuff for the life of him. His father spent *eight* hours studying for a geometry test with him. The child did everything possible to master the material. He received an F anyway. Know what the father did? Gave his son a reward. Appreciated his effort.

Quit riding your daughter on her choice of boyfriend. We weren't such pretty pictures in high school, either. Sure, it would be nice if your daughter's boyfriend, who dreams of being a commercial pilot, hadn't started your high school's first "Frequent Flunker" program, but what can a parent do? Trying to separate people often merely drives them closer.

Times are different! Kids swear, even the good girls and boys. Fashion follows different rules; certain parts of the body are no longer considered private. But, remember: *looking* a certain way and *acting* a certain way can be totally different. If parents assume their children are automatically into trouble, their teens might decide to make that perception reality.

Children are not clones. Just because we dropped the pass in our homecoming game doesn't mean our son has to be a jock. Because we were strong in math, our daughter doesn't need to be an Einstein. We would have resented having to be just like *our* parents. Why wouldn't our kids?

We have to keep the tension to manageable levels, to avoid making the hurtful comment we can never fully take back, to give our child enough freedom so *he learns* responsibility, to not allow our big problems to cause us to belittle.

HOW TO BE A HAPPY PARENT

Remember the movie *Field of Dreams*? A middle-aged man gets a *second* chance to make peace with his father, who died when the son was in his teens. Only in Hollywood. We have but one chance; we dare not blow it.

Recently, my son Bob suffered a mild concussion. He recovered quickly and completely, but for a few minutes in the emergency room, he was unable to speak properly. At such times, everything comes into perspective. You'd give your life for your child to retain the verbal capacity to curse, the physical ability to turn a volume knob on a stereo or throw a new dress over a chair, the initiative to dishonor curfew.

Yes, their doors may be closed, but we must keep the lines of communication open. It was tough for us being teens, and it is tough today. We must set limits, sure, and follow through if behavior is clearly inappropriate. But let's not leave our understanding behind us.

Someday our child will, hopefully, have children. We want to be there for him. For them. At the hospital. To hug the newborn, to feel the tears run down our cheeks and experience that special continuity of family that binds us all.

FRED G. GOSMAN

Such an occasion will provide us with many opportunities: to draw closer to our child; to learn about ourselves; to love a new grandchild.

But it will also allow us to look forward to an especially enjoyable event, which will occur about thirteen years later: when we receive a frantic phone call and our still-precious child complains about *his* teenager.

## Points to Remember

- The more expensive the study desk, the less likely it will be used.

- Teenagers only have patience for those things that are unimportant to their parents.

- Putting excessive pressure on getting good grades is usually counterproductive.

- Alexander Graham Bell *couldn't* have had teenagers.

- The neighbor child always has a later curfew.

- Constantly picking on your teen is a recipe for disaster.

HOW TO BE A HAPPY PARENT

- Children have a right to their own lives; they do not have to relive ours.

- Bad times will pass. It's the relationship that must survive.

# Santa Needs No Hernias

PARENTS NATIONWIDE ARE, INCREASINGLY, asking themselves important questions about Christmas. How can I make the season most meaningful? What's the best way to encourage charitable acts? When did a $49.99 present become a stocking stuffer?

Children's expectations run *high*. An Illinois boy told his parents that he wanted presents that cost "only" $660. When Dad informed him that was about what he anticipated spending on *all* the kids combined, the child retorted that Dad should really think in terms of getting another job.

A seven-year-old Arkansas girl still believes in

Santa. "I have to," she told her mother. "You and Dad couldn't possibly have afforded all these presents."

Belief in Santa makes working with wish lists fairly difficult. Why wouldn't Santa want to make *all* a child's dreams come true? A Maryland couple informs their children that Santa can only bring so many gifts so that he has time to make deliveries to *all* children. An Illinois family threatens to tell Santa "no way" if the gift requested isn't reasonable.

Be *careful* with wish lists. One Ohio mom rues the day she made her biggest mistake, bought *everything* on it. Her youngster was disappointed every succeeding Christmas.

Recently, I heard a suggestion from a mom that seems to make sense. She said her children were *always* disappointed at Christmas because their wish lists built their expectations so high. So she did away with wish lists and surprised the children with their presents, just like on their birthdays. And she says Christmas mornings are now much happier.

Threatening children with no presents if behavior isn't top-notch is rarely effective. One Missouri mom kept threatening and threatening.

Then on Christmas Day her daughter excitedly said to her, "Mommy, Santa came, even though we were bad."

A Kentucky family noticed a marked change in their daughter once she realized who really bought the presents. "She came back and told us she would be thankful for whatever she received and that happiness was the most important thing."

Increasingly, families are putting limits on the number of gifts their children receive. "We give our children *one* special gift at Christmas. It's expensive, but it stands out, and they love it." Large purchases for the family are, increasingly, defined as a gift for *everybody*. Aunts and uncles are encouraged to give joint presents to the nieces and nephews so that the kids aren't buried under a ton of wrapping paper.

Some families limit their children's gifts to three, the number of presents Jesus received from the Wise Men. As a man wrote after hearing me speak at a parochial school, "Perhaps that's why they're called Wise Men."

A Missouri mom now always buys presents at the last minute. Previously, she ran out and made her purchases after each cartoon show. The trouble was, the following week, the children wanted *different* things. So now she waits.

A Michigan mom got tired of the kids always bragging that *their* gifts under the tree were more numerous or larger than those of their siblings. So she numbered the gifts; the children couldn't tell whose was whose. Not only did it solve her problem, but it heightened the kids' anticipation.

Let's remember to give the kids what they want, even if that means fewer presents for a particular child. Too often we buy additional ones, to "even everything up." But if a child really wants an expensive item, what's wrong with making that his only gift if that is what *he* prefers?

Getting a large number of presents on Christmas morning invariably means that the child plays with the few he likes most. Inevitably, the others get lost in the shuffle. One family allows the child to open *half* the presents Christmas morning (he gets to choose which ones) and brings out a present every other week thereafter. Christmas lives on, and the child has more of an opportunity to truly enjoy his new gifts.

Loving family traditions are the highlight of the season in many homes. In Michigan, a father writes each family member a letter, reviewing that person's best actions of the year. He signs it "Santa" and puts it in their stockings. The mom writes, "The children like this better than any present and want it every year, even though now they are older."

Pancakes are the hit in a Colorado home. The family loves to eat them, but all year, Mom limits each family member to three. But on Christmas morning there's no limit. "The children enjoy breakfast as much as their presents."

A Texas family had the kids compose a special song for Christmas. It can *only* be sung on Christmas morning. The kids love it. A New York family makes a special Christmas-tree skirt, decorated with one thing that each family member thinks was important about the past year. And an Illinois mom organizes all the neighborhood kids at Christmastime and helps them prepare a skit for a local nursing home.

My wife created a Valentine's tradition that other families might care to use at Christmas or Chanukah. Since our goldfish had gone to fish heaven, we had two unused goldfish bowls. She filled each bowl with twelve hearts, each entitling a child to a certain treat. For example, "Your Favorite Meal," "Breakfast in Bed," "Let's Rent a

Movie," "Your Choice—Bowling or Miniature Golf." The boys would each select a heart from the bowl on the first of each month. They *loved* it.

Kids are masters at "working over" the grandparents. "Grandma, my other grandma is buying me a train set." So what if the child forgets to mention it's a miniature one? Or, "Grandpa, my other grandpa is buying me one of those devices that allows me to see things better." A microscope? No way. Just a magnifying glass. But who's to know?

Many families are asking different sets of grandparents to specialize, to alternate, so that they aren't in competition with one another. One Christmas, one side gives toys, the other side, clothes. The next Christmas it is reversed. Or the grandparents alternate between giving EE bonds for college, and toys.

Stressing the joy of giving and acts of charity are increasingly common. Many families relate how meaningful it is to their children to save their *own* money to purchase presents. Frequently, parents set up Christmas Club accounts for their kids and even match a certain percentage as a reward for their saving.

Adopting a family and sharing presents with

them is increasingly common. Remember to involve your children directly in your charitable acts. If you are selecting a toy for the "Giving Tree" at school, have your child help select and wrap it.

An Arizona family selects a clothing item for each family member at a resale store and contributes the collective savings to a local charity. One couple takes their son to a nursing center where Mom works so the residents can enjoy his visit. Many parents require children to donate some of their old toys to charity. And I love the policy in a New York home: The child prepares a wish list but also must prepare a "Good-Deeds List," with all projects to be finished before Christmas. A marvelous idea.

And how about the Ohio family where everyone tries to do *anonymous* nice things for one another during the holiday season? Children fold the wash while Mom isn't looking. Sons surreptitiously make their sisters' beds. The kids *love* it!

I am horrible at crossword puzzles, but last year I was doing one and came across the following clue: "A Christmas Chore." And the answer was four letters long. Well, I thought of *shop, bake, wrap*, and then gave up. It depressed me how many answers I could think of.

Making the holiday more meaningful and less stressful increasingly makes sense. Some families visit the relatives in January, to avoid the Christmas rush and to provide a treat in the new year. Many send in-town packages via UPS rather than dropping them off. Some buy cookies rather than baking them. On December 26, more people should be able to say, "What a wonderful Christmas," instead of, "I'm glad that's over for another year."

Families in economic trouble have devised some ingenious strategies. A Wisconsin family had a "rummage" Christmas. Presents were bought during summer rummage sales. The whole extended family got involved. There were no fancy boxes, but people received presents that were initially far more expensive than those they would have otherwise received.

In a Chicago suburb, an entire extended family was in financial trouble. So they declared a "white elephant" Christmas. You could only give as gifts things you already owned. Best Christmas ever. Even the kids loved it. Interesting question, really, as you look around your home for a gift. How much pleasure to give up? How much pleasure to give?

A mom in financial trouble was feeling terribly guilty about spending "only" thirty-five dollars apiece on her three sons. She communicated with the kids and had them select what they really wanted. They bought very wisely. The kids were thankful and happy. Family cooperation can be fostered whatever our budget. Siblings can combine wish lists, wherever possible, and actually learn how to share.

And the traditions of the season can create such precious memories:

In Colorado, two sisters get to select the tree. They can spend *hours* on the lot debating. But they always eventually agree and work *together* to decorate it with homemade ornaments.

And that is one of the greatest gifts of all.

## POINTS TO REMEMBER

- Wish lists should rarely be taller than a child.

- The most-remembered presents are rarely the most expensive.

- The *other* grandmother is always buying a more expensive gift.

- No one child should cause Santa's elves to work overtime.

- The more Christmas gifts a child receives, the less time he will have to appreciate each.

- Doing for others is the best way to get children to stop thinking just of themselves.

- Charitable acts at Christmas should be a *family* undertaking.

- Family Christmas traditions, not presents, are what children will recall most fondly.

# When in Doubt, Relax

WORRY, WORRY, WORRY! SUCH IS THE LIFE of parents.

I know a couple that checks on *everything*. Looks in on the baby forty-five times a night. Tests the middle son's cholesterol level every other week. Hires a private detective to do a background check on every potential sitter.

The world is a scary place. Sure, we have to worry some, but not about *everything*. Some things take care of themselves. Your child will:

be potty-trained by middle school
adjust to the new sibling
stop sucking his thumb

give up the bottle by kindergarten
stay seated for an entire meal
sleep through the night
go to parties without crying
eventually drive slower

We'll still have enough to worry about. The mother of the class brain wishes her child were more social. Meanwhile, the father of the most popular kid in class wishes his child would pay more attention to academics.

Same with age differences. If our kids are close in age, we regret their competitiveness. But if the age span is substantial, we wish they had more in common.

Kids change. The shy one becomes the politician; the docile one, a debater. The messy child becomes a neat freak. So why fret while the jury is still out?

We could be more relaxed if we remembered that every problem isn't *our* problem. A mother overheard a child teasing her daughter about her "Korean eyes." Mom was about to pounce. Then she overheard her daughter calmly say, "You're just jealous because you can't have them."

Homework is the *child's* responsibility. Sure, we

want to remind him about it and help with it. But, bottom line, it is *his* job, and making it ours teaches nothing meaningful. A mom stayed up until three in the morning drawing charts for a report her son had left to the last minute. In the morning, her child complained about their quality. She writes, "It was the last report I ever did."

If your child promised to mow a neighbor's lawn, remind him once or twice about it. But then if he forgets, let *him* bear the consequences. Or if your daughter fails to return the rented videos, let *her* pay the fine.

A mom required one of her three boys to carry down the hamper on wash day, and the boys took turns. One week, they argued over whose turn it was, and the hamper stayed put. How easy it would have been for Mom to bail out the kids. But she refused. "The problem was quickly solved when the boys had to wear dirty clothes to school due to *their* irresponsibility."

It would be nice if every decision we made was bound to be the correct one, but this can't be. So why expect it? Professional baseball players hit .300 and are pleased. If they can fail seven out of ten times, why can't we accept an occasional miscue?

### HOW TO BE A HAPPY PARENT

We sing along with our child to Big Bird's, "Everybody Makes Mistakes So Why Not You?" We should remember that the message applies to us old folks, too. My father had a favorite expression: "If I knew I'd die in Chicago, I'd stay in Milwaukee." Hindsight is always twenty-twenty. It's a luxury we parents lack.

Chance plays such a big role in life. Who knows what's best? Once, the mother of baseball great Bob Feller surprised him and went to the ballpark on Mother's Day to watch him pitch. She was struck by a foul ball and was hospitalized for two weeks. As Bob Feller relates, "I went the full nine innings, but *Mom* did not."

Bill Gates, founder of Microsoft, dropped out of college. Now he's one of the world's richest men. Our kids should do so well.

A right-handed child broke his arm, and it had to be set in a cast. Shortly after the cast was removed, the child broke it again. Throughout this time the youngster learned to throw left-handed. Now he's one of the top pitching prospects in the country.

John Ratzenberger, who played Cliff on *Cheers*, figured the TV series "would never go more than seven episodes." So who's to know? A man in

Chicago is alive because a bullet deflected off of a lighter he had in his pocket. Where would he be today if his mother insisted that he never smoke?

Even knowing if a child is lying is difficult. In New Jersey, a child was accused by a teacher of hitting a fellow student. The youngster *swore* to the teacher that he was innocent. The teacher believed him, saying that after twenty-five years' experience, he could always tell if a child was lying. Mom and child walked back to the car. But when the child sat down, he whispered to Mom, "I really did hit her!"

Spending hours researching strategies isn't a panacea, either. Experts often disagree, so which do you believe? Theories change over time. The information alone can cause anxiety. Have you seen all those commercials listing the ten warning signs of depression? I get panicky every time; I'm convinced everyone in America suffers from at least seven of the symptoms.

Often, our best efforts only produce *more* stress for our child. Let's say he will be attending a new school. We have him visit six times with a psychologist who specializes in family moves. Buy him his own copy of *Surviving a New School*. Require him to memorize the names of everyone who will be in his class. So, tell me, why in the world would our child be relaxed on his first day of school?

We can't devote ourselves *exclusively* to our kids. We need time by ourselves, or with our spouse or friends, to clear our head and adjust our attitude. Too many couples forgo this "alone time," especially if Mom works during the week, and routinely devote Friday *and* Saturday night to the kids.

If you can't afford a sitter, ask Grandma or another relative to help out occasionally. Or alternate with friends: You mind their children one weekend; they reciprocate the next. Children need attention, no question, but so do adults. We *need* time away. How sad it is to discover late in life that the children have blossomed but a marriage has withered.

But even with recharged batteries, problems will occur. We can't run from them. When Bob and Mike were very young, a friend's daughter spent the night. Everything seemingly went well, but then things got interesting. The next day, we discovered one of the boys had head lice. So we had to call the girl's parents and let them know.

More was to come. The following day, we discovered that one of the boys had pinworm. On the phone again to the girl's folks. Tough calls to make. The parents took it well, but their daughter seemed to develop a preference for her own bed.

Don't be scared by momentary crises. It's the nineties; we all have them. Talk to your friends and relatives. They probably have firsthand experience with the problem. We won't know if we keep our mouths shut.

We shouldn't always expect the worst. A Pennsylvania four-year-old confided to her mother that she knew what "you and Daddy were doing last night after I went to sleep." Mom frantically thought of responses to the anticipated questions about sex. Instead, her daughter said, "You and Daddy had ice cream, 'cause I saw the dishes in the sink."

A concerned father took his five-year-old daughter to the ophthalmologist. She had been blinking excessively. A hundred dollars later the ophthalmologist informed the dad that his daughter had mastered the art of flirting.

Many of us have lives that turned out differently from our childhood dreams. Some working women daily go to work feeling guilty about not being at home. How harmful! Not good for Mom,

HOW TO BE A HAPPY PARENT

Dad, or the kids. *We have to accept our realities.* It would be horrible if our children felt constant guilt. So too for us parents.

Same with divorce. It happens. Years ago, our child might have been the only "child of divorce" in his school. Today, it's practically the majority of kids. Divorce is terribly sad and traumatic. But life continues. And when half the class has gone through a similar situation, the pain has to be somewhat less for our children.

Let's remember that parenting is an art, not a science. Take two kids from the same home. One might turn out terrific; the other, not so terrific. So who's to know?

We just have to relax and do our best. We take pride when we give *others* the benefit of the doubt, second chances. Aren't we ourselves entitled to equal consideration?

There are no perfect parents. Oh, I've heard rumors that they exist. You know, irritating people who can quote the percentage of real-juice content in every fruit drink on the market or who take an equal number of pictures of their second child. I've just never met any.

We have to give ourselves credit for all the many wonderful things we do for our children.

FRED G. GOSMAN

Once I was buying an ice cream cone and a mom asked for a sample of the caramel. That was her son's favorite flavor, and she was sampling it at three different places so she would know where to buy it for his birthday party. A tad excessive, perhaps, but if the mom has time for the research, why not? But how can such a mom ever question whether she is doing enough for her child?

I was excessive once with a pair of Mike's sneakers. They were wet, and my wife asked me at 1:00 A.M. to put them in the dryer. Well, because the heavy shoes were flying around inside, the dryer kept shutting off every fifteen seconds. What to do? Go to sleep? A temptation, but then I had a vision of the *scene*. You know, the *scene*. We all have it, in one form or another. Mike wears wet shoes to school. He develops pneumonia. Medicine proves ineffective. And his last words to me are, "Dad, why didn't you lose a little sleep and dry my shoes?" So I hit the sack at two-thirty.

Caring parents do *so much* for their kids. Dad constructs the cradle from scratch, and Mom spends eighteen months selecting the perfect car seat. We kiss away thousands of owies and walk our babies miles when they are sick. We sit through a ninety-minute lecture on the differences among natural, latex, and silicone nipples. Refuse to buy a home within four miles of an electromagnetic field. Quiz our daughter's T-ball coach for three hours on his philosophy of winning. Stay home from work to introduce ourselves to our son's bus driver. Never buy a baby book prior to reading six reviews. Study the fire evacuation plans of ten potential nursery schools. Throw ourselves in front of a departing ice cream wagon so that our daughter gets the cone she will never finish.

If you have paid your dues, it is time to relax, to feel good about yourself. John Wooden, former basketball coach at UCLA, once said, "There is no pillow as soft as a clear conscience."

It is advice that applies both on and off the court.

### Points to Remember

- Today's vegetable hater is tomorrow's avocado rancher.

- Just because there's a decision doesn't mean there's a crisis.

- Baby-sitters are a parent's best friend.

FRED G. GOSMAN

- Comparing your child constantly with other children is the quickest path to insecurity.

- We don't expect perfection from our children; remember not to expect it from yourself.

- Your neighbor's home is as dysfunctional as yours.

- Parents need occasional quality time *away* from children in order to have consistent quality time *with* children.

# Conclusion

**I**T IS TIME TO SIMPLIFY OUR PARENTING. To trust our own instincts. To use plain old common sense. To believe in ourselves again.

Caring parents are united on many things. We know we should worry less and enjoy our kids more. We're tired of feeling guilty saying no. We admit that three-hundred-dollar birthday parties and hundred-dollar tennis shoes aren't producing happier children.

We don't want our teenagers at motels after proms. And we fear that our children's future will be tougher than ours was, and *want* to instill a work ethic and appreciation of the value of money so they will thrive. In short, we are ready for change.

But we can't let our minds talk us out of it. They play tricks, you know. My father used to walk three miles a day. One Father's Day I bought him a pedometer, to measure how far he walked. Well, Dad tried it out and loved it. He was in great spirits, felt *invigorated* from his three-mile walk. But when he told me where he had gone, I became concerned that the pedometer was defective and that he had walked too far. We retraced his route in the car, and Dad had walked *seven* miles. Instantly, he felt *exhausted*.

Let's remember that change can often be slow. Back when Dr. James Naismith hung a peach basket on a balcony of a gym, inventing basketball, someone had to climb a ladder to remove the ball from the basket after each goal. It was *twenty-nine* years before someone thought to cut the bottom off the basket.

We must focus on the immeasurable joys children provide. The hugs. The kisses. The thoughtfulness. In New York a traveling father arrived home to hear his son say, "I missed you so much I used your toothbrush." An Illinois daughter offered her piggy bank when she learned Mom was unemployed. A mom and dad who sent their son to space camp received flowers from him addressed to "the best parents a child could ever have."

And the humor! The girl who placed thirty white stones under her pillow to "trick the tooth fairy." The Long Island eleven-year-old who called home *collect* to complain about the cheese sandwich. The son who came home with flowers for Mom picked at a nearby field, a cemetery. The daughter, denied television, who threatened to "show and tell" on her parents. And the East Coast four-year-old who pleaded with Mom to buy the Batman figure because "life is too short."

And let's not forget the wondrous innocence. That encourages us. Keeps us on balance. Once Mike and I were building a birdhouse. I didn't follow the directions precisely, and things didn't fit. In frustration, I banged the birdhouse on the table, making it an even more humorous sight. Then young Mike looked at it and said, "What a pretty birdhouse." I quickly regained my composure and finished the funny-looking thing.

We must give our children our best. But we

also must accept our imperfections, and be realistic in what we can accomplish. And give ourselves credit.

When my wife was pregnant with Bob, our oldest, I decided to knit a baby blanket. I went out and bought the prettiest and softest pink and blue yarn I could find.

My mother-in-law gave me a quick lesson, and I diligently worked for many, many hours. Unfortunately, I set the craft back a hundred years. I was so afraid of dropping stitches that I kept *adding* them. Knitted the world's first *trapezoidal* baby blanket.

I suppose I should have been terribly embarrassed by it, and hidden it in some drawer. But I must confess nothing made me feel prouder or happier than seeing our precious new son wrapped in it.

I hoped it would keep him warm. I hoped it would keep him safe.

And I hoped he could feel the love.

# Time to Share

THIS BOOK WOULD NOT HAVE BEEN POSSIBLE without the thousands of suggestions volunteered from homes across America. Will you share, too?

What is the funniest thing your child ever said? The most embarrassing situation you ever found yourself in? Your most ingenious tactic? Your biggest challenge as a parent? I'd love to use these in my next book.

Please send your stories and comments to me, Fred Gosman, P.O. Box 11558, Milwaukee, WI 53211. You can also use this address to contact me about speaking before your association, or parent, educational, or corporate group. Or reach me directly at 414-241-3005.

Thanks!

ABOUT THE AUTHOR

FRED G. GOSMAN, father of two teenagers, lives in Milwaukee, Wisconsin, and speaks nationally on a wide variety of parenting and educational issues.